THE BIRDS KEEP ON SINGING

STEPHEN COCKETT

Series Consultant
Cecily O'Neil

Collins Educational
An Imprint of HarperCollins*Publishers*

Published by Collins Educational
77-85 Fulham Palace Road, London W6 8JB
An imprint of HarperCollins*Publishers*

ISBN 000 330315 2

Designed by Wendi Watson
Cover design by Chi Leung
Cover photograph Imperial War Museum
Commissioning Editor Domenica de Rosa
Editor Louisa Coulthurst
Production Susan Cashin
Printed in Hong Kong

Acknowledgements
The following publishers, authors and agents are thanked for
permission to reproduce extracts and copyright material:
Bloomsbury Publishing for the extract from *No Time to Wave
Goodbye* by Ben Wicks pp88, 89, 90, 91, 92, 94, 96, 107.
Ebury Press for the extract from *War Factory – Mass Observation* by
Celia Fremlin p81.
Penguin Books for the extracts from *Living Through The Blitz* by
Tom Harrisson p98.
Peters, Fraser and Dunlop Group and HarperCollins*Publishers* for
the extracts from *War Wives* by Colin and Eileen Townsend pp93,
102-3, 104.

The following are thanked for permission to reproduce photographs:
HarperCollins*Publishers* pp101, 102.
Hulton Getty Picture Collection Limited pp79, 82.
Imperial War Museum pp74, 76, 80, 100.
Popperfoto pp91, 93, 97

Every effort has been made to contact owners of copyright material
but if any have been inadvertently overlooked the publishers will be
pleased to make the necessary arrangements at the first opportunity.

CONTENTS

THE CHARACTERS

The play is set in the outskirts of a small town about 30 miles south of Manchester, during the Second World War.

Evacuees from Manchester:

MRS PARKS – mid-thirties
    She is evacuated with her children to make sure they are properly cared for, but feels out of place away from her home and husband.

ROSIE PARKS – daughter, age 13
    Intelligent and resourceful. Suspicious of Terry.

BEN PARKS – son, age 11
    Less mature than his sister, and easily influenced by Terry.

TERRY HUDSON – age 13
    An evacuee from a poor part of Manchester. There is something secretive and menacing about him.

LIAM – the Parks children's uncle, early thirties
    A soldier in the British army, evacuated from Dunkirk. He has an appealing good humour which conceals his anxiety about returning to the war.

Residents in the town:

PEGGY – late twenties
    She has been married for only a short time to Danny who is away fighting in the war. She hates the war for shattering her expectations of domestic bliss.

ANGIE – Peggy's sister, early twenties
    She is single and sees the war as an exciting opportunity to do something in her life with a real purpose. Though different from Peggy, she gets on well with her.

BILLETING OFFICER

AIR RAID PRECAUTION WARDEN

Evacuees from London:

GLORIA DAWKINS – late twenties
    Worked in a London hotel until the bombs came. She is attractive and well-dressed and has a sense of humour similar to Liam's.

MARGARET – Gloria's niece, aged 13
    Shy and reserved. On her arrival she is still partly in shock from her experience of the war in London, but quickly makes friends with Rosie.

THE BIRDS KEEP ON SINGING

At one end of the acting area is Peggy's house which has a large kitchen. The room, though quite ordinary, looks cared for by a house proud person. At the side of the acting area is the front door which gives access both to the kitchen and to stairs to a bedroom on a higher level. In the bedroom, there are two beds and a chest of drawers.

At the opposite end of the acting area is Allsprings House. There is a sign for Allsprings House which suggests a grand property set in large grounds. There is a basement which is dark and contains a variety of junk. Steps from the basement lead up to a door and a passageway where there is also a door to a wine cellar.

There is no fixed boundary line between the two locations. At the back of the stage is a screen for projecting pictures. Music of the period is heard as the audience enters. The play begins with the following sequence of pictures and voices.

Picture: the Prime Minister, Neville Chamberlain.

CHAMBERLAIN   '...unless we heard from them by 11 o'clock that they were prepared at once to withdraw their troops from Poland, that a state of war would exist between us. I have to tell you now, that no such undertaking has been received, and that, consequently, this country is at war with Germany.'

Pictures: evacuees leaving home, walking to the stations, travelling on the trains, arriving at reception centres.

BBC COMMENTATOR   'The evacuation of British children is going on smoothly and efficiently. The Ministry of Health says that great progress has been made with the first part of the government's arrangements. Railways, the road transport organisations, the local authorities and teachers, the voluntary workers, and not least, the householders in the reception areas, are all playing their parts splendidly.'

During this commentary, a dim light comes up on **Terry** *in the bedroom of Peggy's house. He is looking out of a window in the 'invisible wall' towards Allsprings House. Lights pick out the Allsprings sign and the contour of the objects in the basement.* **Terry** *looks unkempt and poorly dressed. His gaze is fixed and intense.*

Picture: Winston Churchill.

CHURCHILL   'I have formed an administration of men and women of every party, and almost every point of view. We have differed and quarrelled in the past, but now one band unites us all, to wage war until victory is won, and never to surrender ourselves to servitude and shame, whatever the cost of the agony may be.'

Picture: German troops.

BBC ANNOUNCER (ALVAR LIDEL)   'This is the BBC Home Service. The German Army invaded Holland and Belgium early this morning by land and by landings from parachutes. The armies of the Low Countries are resisting. An appeal for help has been made to the allied governments, and Brussels says that allied troops are moving to their support.'

Music and pictures continue.

The Billeting Officer enters followed by Mrs Parks, Rosie and Ben with their suitcases. The light is dim and their words cannot be heard above the music. The Billeting Officer asks them to wait, then goes off towards Peggy's house. A brief tableau of the Parks family, Terry at the window, and a picture of evacuees on the screen.

SCENE ONE

*The kitchen in Peggy's House. **Peggy** and **Angie** are arguing. The **Billeting Officer** keeps a discreet distance.*

PEGGY   No!

ANGIE   Why not?

PEGGY   We've got one already, and look at the state of him. That was your idea, too.

ANGIE   We can't just have one.

PEGGY   He counts for two, and that was our limit. We agreed.

ANGIE   Think of the war effort.

PEGGY   Don't war effort me. I never asked for any evacuees. *To the Billeting Officer* A good thing you've come. I want you to find another billet for that Terry up there.

ANGIE   Peggy!

PEGGY   He smells. He doesn't know what a toilet is, and he's trouble. I can't cope with all that and do my job at the factory, war or no war. *Pause* And what's she doing with them?

ANGIE   She's their mother.

PEGGY   Mothers as well? They never told us that.

BILLETING OFFICER   We weren't expecting mothers with the older ones.

ANGIE   But it will be better this way. She'll look after them. It might even be easier than Terry on his own.

Pause.

PEGGY   They're not coming unless Terry goes. Finding one place should be easier than finding three. *To the **Billeting Officer*** What about it then?

BILLETING OFFICER   There aren't enough places as it is. I don't know what I'm going to do.

ANGIE   We can't leave them standing out there. They must be tired and worried.

She makes a move to get the Parks family.

PEGGY   Angie, this is my house, not yours. I decide.

ANGIE   Peggy, there's a war on. It's not up to us to decide. We do what we're asked. I'm going to get them.

PEGGY   *desperate* They're not coming in here.

ANGIE   Don't worry, I'm here to help you.

PEGGY   Help, you call it?

Angie goes out. Peggy feels beaten. She sits at the table and puts her head in her hands. Angie brings the Parks family into the house and takes them upstairs.

BILLETING OFFICER   She your sister?

PEGGY   Yes.

BILLETING OFFICER   Knows her own mind, doesn't she?

PEGGY   The army's made for her. She'll go far.

BILLETING OFFICER   Living here?

PEGGY   My husband's away in the army, and she's staying here while she trains over at the Barracks. It seemed like a good idea when she suggested it.

Pause.

BILLETING OFFICER   You're right about that Terry . He has a shifty look. Noticed that myself when I first saw him. No label on him, like the rest of them. Or a change of clothes. Something funny there. Anyway, he told us his address and we're making a few enquiries. As soon as something comes up, I'll let you know.

PEGGY   A new billet for him would be better.

BILLETING OFFICER   I'll see what I can do. Bye.

She leaves. Lights cross fade to the bedroom.

SCENE TWO

The bedroom in Peggy's House. Terry is still looking out of the window at Allsprings House. Rosie, Ben and Mrs Parks are looking at the room. Though not particularly well dressed, they look much smarter than Terry.

ANGIE   I'll show you the rooms first so you can take up your cases. Then we'll have some tea. This is Terry. He's been here a couple of days. Terry, Ben and... *tries to remember Rosie's name*

ROSIE   Rosie.

ANGIE   Rosie. And Mrs Parks. They're evacuees from Manchester, too. We need another bed for Ben. A camp bed. You have it, Terry. Ben and Rosie can have these two beds.

TERRY *eyeing Ben* He's not having my bed. I got here first.

ANGIE Drawers for clothes in this chest. Anything you can't fit in, put under the bed.

TERRY *to Ben* Over here's mine. You're not to come past that line in the floor there.

Pause.

ANGIE *going over to the 'window'* You're high up here. See the view?

Rosie and Ben come over and look through the 'window'. Mrs Parks starts to unpack their cases. Terry stands back but keeps an eye on Rosie and Ben.

BEN Cor! What's that place? The big house, there?

ANGIE Allsprings House.

ROSIE Who lives there?

ANGIE Mr Forbes-Lomax.

ROSIE Who's he?

ANGIE Everybody round here knows Mr Forbes-Lomax. Well, **who** he is. The Lord of the Manor, something like that.

BEN Who else lives there?

ANGIE Just him.

ROSIE On his own. In that big house?

ANGIE Not even him now. He's gone off to the war.

BEN A soldier?

ANGIE The house is beautiful. Behind the trees there's a lake with flowers all around and swans on the water.

ROSIE What about his family?

ANGIE He never married, so he has no children.

ROSIE Must be lonely for him.

ANGIE He has lots of friends, though. You should see his parties. Lots of people, ladies in fine dresses, music, big cars parked right down the driveway. He also goes to London a lot to see friends. He owns a big hotel there.

BEN Does he have any servants?

ANGIE They've all gone. Mr Forbes-Lomax shut up the house as soon as the war started.

BEN Where is he, in the war?

ANGIE Not been heard of since the day he left. In France probably.

TERRY He's a soldier. *Rosie and Ben turn to look at Terry* Like my dad.

5

ANGIE   Your dad's away too?
TERRY   He's a sniper.

Pause.

ANGIE   See over there, on the other side of the estate? Those are the Barracks where I'm doing my training.
BEN   *to **Angie*** Are you a soldier, too?
ANGIE   Sort of. The Auxiliary Territorial Service. For women.
TERRY   Women can't be soldiers.
ANGIE   Maybe in this war they can, Terry.

Pause.

ROSIE   Is it going to stay empty, the big house?
ANGIE   Not for long. Some other evacuees are coming. Mr Forbes-Lomax said they could use the house during the war for as long as they like.
BEN   Cor! Live there?
ROSIE   *enthusiastically* They'll be able to live like Lords and Ladies. Can we see inside?
ANGIE   Perhaps when they arrive, they'll show you round. The Billeting Officer is expecting them anytime.
BEN   They'll be able to have posh parties too.
ANGIE   *to **Mrs Parks*** All finished?
MRS PARKS   Nearly.
ANGIE   Your room's downstairs. I'll show you to it, then perhaps you'd like to come downstairs and meet my sister, Peggy.
MRS PARKS   *to **Rosie** and **Ben*** We'll call you in a few minutes.
ANGIE   *to the children* I have to be back at the Barracks soon, but I'll be popping in and out. Bye.
ROSIE   Bye.

*Angie goes out. There is a long silence while **Terry** looks at **Rosie** and **Ben,** and they at him.*

TERRY   There's a way in.
ROSIE   What?
TERRY   The house. Over there.
BEN   You've been inside?
TERRY   'Course I have.
ROSIE   Break in?
TERRY   Didn't need to.

BEN   On your own?

TERRY   No with the army, stupid.

ROSIE   How?

TERRY   Easy.

ROSIE   But how?

TERRY   It's secret. Nobody will ever find out how.

BEN   What's in there?

TERRY   That would be telling.

BEN   You been in all the rooms?

TERRY   Everywhere.

ROSIE   That's trespassing.

TERRY   No it's not. We're evacuees.

ROSIE   So what?

TERRY   He said we could. The owner, Mr Forbes. He said evacuees could use it.

ROSIE   Not us, though. Others.

Pause.

TERRY   Do you want to go in there, or don't you?

BEN   You'd show us the secret way in?

TERRY   Stupid. I'd have to, wouldn't I?

BEN   *to* **Rosie** Shall we?

Pause.

TERRY   You wait till you see what's in there. It's a special place.

Pause.

BEN   Let's do it, Rosie.

ROSIE   You might be telling lies.

TERRY   One way of finding out. *Pause* Well, are you coming, or not?

BEN   Now?

TERRY   We go now and they'll be suspicious. Tomorrow, when they're out or doing something.

BEN   *eagerly to* **Rosie** Rosie?

As **Rosie** *considers her decision, the lights fade.*

Pictures of Dunkirk, troops on the beaches, coming ashore in England. Radio commentary.

COMMENTATOR   'For days and nights, ships of all kinds have plied to and fro across the channel under the fierce onslaught of the enemy bombers, utterly regardless of the perils, to bring out as many as possible of the trapped British Expeditionary Force. There was every kind of ship that I saw coming in this morning, and every one of them was crammed full of tired, battle-stained and bloodstained British soldiers.'

SCENE THREE

*The kitchen in Peggy's House, the following day. The sun shines through the window. **Peggy** is cleaning and polishing the room. There is a pile of washing on the table. **Mrs Parks** enters, takes off her coat and hangs it on a hook by the door.*

MRS PARKS   Oh! I wasn't expecting you back from work so soon.

PEGGY   The charge hand sent me home. I was falling asleep at the machine.

MRS PARKS   Like some tea?

PEGGY   No thanks. The pot's fresh.

Mrs Parks gets herself a cup of tea.

MRS PARKS   The children seem to be settling in. They all went out together. Across to the gardens. I hope it's all right.

PEGGY   It's a safe place for them to play. Forbes-Lomax won't be worrying about his flower borders.

MRS PARKS   I'm not sure about Terry. He looks like he might be a bad influence.

PEGGY   With a bit of luck, he'll have a new billet soon. *She continues to work.* Slave labour it is at the factory. Sometimes I think I'll go crazy, drilling holes in metal plates all day. Must have done a million by now. I even dream about them.

Pause.

MRS PARKS   Shouldn't you be resting?

PEGGY   Putting the place in order calms me down. Why did I ever let her talk me into it?

MRS PARKS   Angie?

PEGGY   'You need to earn some money...' Well, that's true, – 'and give yourself a purpose while Danny's away, occupy your mind'. Goodness, a mind's the last thing you need for what I'm doing. *Pause* And then it's got to be something to do with the war effort, but tough luck, the factory happens to be three miles away. So, it's a six mile bus journey each day. *Realising she is going on a bit* I'm sorry.

MRS PARKS   No, no, I understand.

PEGGY   More tea? *She tops up both cups.* Actually, it's not the work so much as the attitude. That charge hand – Popeye with the bulging eyes – well, he needs a spanner where it hurts. Like yesterday, my machine got stuck, so I called him over to sort it out and he says 'you've put the drill in crooked. You in love or something?' And like a fool I said, 'this machine doesn't seem to like me', so then he says 'it don't like anybody who can't use it right. No mechanical sense, that's what's the matter with you girls, no mechanical sense.' *Pause* He wouldn't talk like that to a man.

Pause.

MRS PARKS   Like something to eat?

PEGGY   I couldn't just yet. Thanks.

Silence. Peggy looks around the kitchen. She gets up, runs her finger along a ledge.

PEGGY   Look at that. Dust everywhere.

She takes out dusters and polish and starts cleaning and tidying. **Mrs Parks** *sorts and folds the washing.* **Peggy** *stops for a moment and watches her.*

PEGGY   You didn't have to come here. You could have stayed in Manchester and sent the children with all the other evacuees.

MRS PARKS   I wanted to be sure where they were...that they were happy. Now that they are here, I can't think why I worried. Actually, I...

PEGGY   Listen, I should apologise.

MRS PARKS   What for?

PEGGY   It was very rude of me...not to give you a better welcome.

MRS PARKS   We're asking a lot of you. It's a great relief to me that the children are here. I was expecting the worst.

Pause.

PEGGY   What does your husband do?

MRS PARKS   He's an electronics engineer at Vickers in Manchester. Something to do with radar.

PEGGY   At least you know where he is. This is all I've got. *She takes a letter from the mantelpiece* One letter after he got to France. Since then, nothing.

MRS PARKS   In wartime...

Peggy takes a framed photograph and polishes it.

PEGGY   This was taken soon after we were married about a year ago.

MRS PARKS   *looking at the picture* It must be hard, not getting any letters.

Peggy returns the photograph to its place and arranges and polishes the mantelpiece.

PEGGY   It makes me angry about the war. I only ever wanted to be a housewife. Silly, isn't it, but I actually like cleaning and cooking, and making the house look like it's worth coming home to. I'd got the future nicely sorted out, and the war's ruined it all. Danny's on some sort of special mission. Could be anywhere. I send letters to him all the time so it won't seem strange when he comes back, but they can't be getting through. I'd like him to know that I'm keeping the house just as it was for when he gets back. *Pause* Terry's thrown the plan a bit.

MRS PARKS   Where's he from?

PEGGY   Manchester somewhere. The Billeting Officer is making some enquiries. She'll let us know as soon as she hears anything.

Pause.

MRS PARKS   I've just been out to the telephone.

PEGGY   Everything all right?

MRS PARKS   Fine, fine. Well, apart from my brother-in-law who's back from Dunkirk. He's wounded, nothing too serious, but he has to rest for a while. Not a lot of fun for him. He lives on his own, you see. *Pause* Peggy, there is something I need to ask you.

Angie enters in uniform for the first time.

ANGIE   It's done, finished.

PEGGY   The war?

10

ANGIE   My initial training. What do you think?

PEGGY   Think?

ANGIE   The uniform.

PEGGY   It certainly makes you look more like the real thing.

ANGIE   Interviews for special training tomorrow. I've told them I won't do a job in an office or something like sparkplug testing. I want a real job.

PEGGY   And what might that be?

ANGIE   Radar operator, mechanic, driver, range finder, anti-aircraft gunner.

PEGGY   Angie , this is a war, you know. People get killed. You don't have to volunteer.

ANGIE   I don't, but I will. *Peggy shakes her head* Peggy, I've spent the last four years of my life selling knitting needles and buttons in a draper's shop, advising overweight ladies on corsets to improve the figure, and measuring up for loose covers. I can't say I wanted this war, but I'm going to make the most of it. Please don't try to stop me.

Pause.

PEGGY   So what's the next move in your plan of campaign?

ANGIE   To sort out my washing. *She looks through the pile of washing and picks out her things* Where are the towels?

PEGGY   Still on the line. Don't worry, I'll get them for you.

Peggy and Angie go out. Mrs Parks is left alone.

SCENE FOUR

The hall in Allsprings House. Rosie and Ben and Terry are lit by sunlight through a stained glass window. Terry is gazing at a portrait of Mr Forbes-Lomax.

BEN   It's like church.

ROSIE   I've seen a film like this. With a big staircase and curtains...Shirley Temple...the one where she tap dances all the way down, with music...

BEN   *testing the acoustics* Oi! *Waits* Here that echo?

ROSIE   Shut up, will you! Somebody'll hear us.

BEN Who?
ROSIE The Billeting Officer?
BEN Nah!
TERRY That's him. Look.

Terry's gaze remains fixed on one of the portraits.

BEN Who?
TERRY Mr Forbes-Lomax.
BEN In the painting?
TERRY Always asking questions, you are.
BEN The one who's gone to the war?
TERRY You're doing it again.
ROSIE *looking at other paintings* It's got to be him. See the others, they're older.
TERRY He looks like a soldier.
ROSIE Reminds me of...
TERRY In charge of a regiment, I'll bet.
ROSIE ...that film star...what's his name?
TERRY A leader. *Pause* Got courage, you can tell.
ROSIE How can you, from a picture?
TERRY I can. And anyway, I know.
ROSIE What do you mean, you know?
TERRY All his family are soldiers. War heroes.
ROSIE Get off, Terry.
TERRY I'll show you.

Terry leads them to another room.

BEN Uniforms!

All three face the audience on one side of the acting area. They are looking into a large display case with a glass front.

TERRY See?
ROSIE *reading an inscription* 'Uniforms of the Great European Powers.'
TERRY He collects 'em.
ROSIE '...all the uniforms...worn by soldiers on active service.'
BEN Eh?
TERRY They fought battles wearing these uniforms.
BEN Doesn't make him a war hero. Collecting uniforms.
TERRY Shut up, Ben.
ROSIE 'Light Infantryman P J Dawson...Relief of Ma-fe-king.'

BEN Where's that?

ROSIE Don't know.

BEN *laughing* Look at that one with the brush on top.

ROSIE 'Helmut' somebody. Chief Gunnery Officer on the German destroyer...

BEN *laughing* Helmut's helmet.

ROSIE ...Jutland.

TERRY See this photograph?

ROSIE 'Henry Forbes-Lomax.'

BEN Hey, that's like the man in the painting.

TERRY Not him, stupid. Look again.

ROSIE 'Henry Forbes-Lomax. King's College, Cambridge. Born 1887. Died 1st July 1916. The Battle of the Somme.'

BEN Is that his uniform?

TERRY Or one like it.

BEN Who was he?

TERRY Who do you think?

BEN The brother of the man in the painting?

Terry scoffs.

ROSIE His father.

Pause.

TERRY See? *Pause* I can show you something even better. *Ben and Rosie look at him, their interest held* Follow me.

They follow Terry out.

SCENE FIVE

The kitchen in Peggy's House. Peggy is preparing to leave for work. Mrs. Parks is sitting at the table.

PEGGY I've got to be off or I'll miss the bus. Popeye rearranged my shift. You can have a rest, you see, but only long enough to keep you awake at the bench. He'll be standing at the gate with his watch, you can be sure of it.

Angie enters, still on a search for washing. She is rather grim faced about it. Peggy watches her for a moment.

PEGGY You'd better tell them you don't want a job in the laundry, either.

ANGIE   Funny.

She goes out.

MRS PARKS   Peggy...before you go...I need to ask you something.

PEGGY   *suddenly remembering* Goodness. I got side-tracked. What is it?

MRS PARKS   Peggy, I'm in two minds about this evacuation business. I came with Rosie and Ben to be sure they were all right, but, now I'm here, I feel I need to be at home. Which is worse, the threat of the bombs or splitting up the family? I'm torn. I can't say anything to the children, they'll get upset. It's hard enough for them as it is. *Pause* You've been very good to us. *Pause* Peggy...I was thinking...my brother-in-law...Liam...I mentioned him earlier...the one who was brought back wounded from Dunkirk...perhaps he could stay here and I go back to Manchester for a while. The children will love having him around. He's their favourite uncle and I know I can trust him to look after them.

PEGGY   Well, I don't know. A soldier in the house. I hadn't expected that. What next?

MRS PARKS   Just for a short time and then I'll sort things out, one way or the other.

PEGGY   If he's wounded, doesn't he need a hospital?

MRS PARKS   It's nothing very serious and he's been home quite a while already. Just a bit of rest is all he needs. The army will want him back soon, anyway.

PEGGY   Really, Mrs Parks...if I'd known...

MRS PARKS   It's hardly fair of me to ask you, I know.

Pause.

PEGGY   Angie'll be pleased. They'll be able to talk war together.

MRS PARKS   I do appreciate this. We don't have a telephone at home but I could give you my neighbour's number in case you need to get in touch.

PEGGY   Might be easier with Terry, having a man around.

MRS PARKS   If you don't mind, I'll let them know straight away.

*She goes out. **Peggy** remains seated. **Angie** enters looking apologetic.*

ANGIE   All sorted.

PEGGY   Why the sudden concern about washing?

Angie sits down with her at the table.

ANGIE   From tomorrow we have to be prepared to be
  posted at a moment's notice.
PEGGY   Why?
ANGIE   If I can't do my special training here, I have to
move to another camp.
PEGGY   You never said.
ANGIE   I didn't know.
PEGGY   Can't you choose something you can do here?
ANGIE   We'll see. It may not happen. *She gets up* I have
  to go back to the Barracks.

*She goes out. **Peggy** sits for a moment in silence. She turns to
look at the photograph on the mantelpiece, then goes out.*

SCENE SIX

*The basement room in Allsprings House. **Terry** enters the
passageway outside the room, followed by **Ben** and **Rosie**.*

TERRY   *facing the door* This is it.
BEN   *pushes the door* Locked.

Terry takes out a large key.

ROSIE   Where did you get that?
TERRY   In the kitchen. On a hook.
BEN   *pointing down the passageway* What's that room
  there?
TERRY   That's nothing. It's full of bottles on shelves.
ROSIE   His wine cellar.
BEN   His what?
ROSIE   He keeps his wine in there. All posh houses have
  wine cellars.

*Terry unlocks the door and switches on the light, a single bulb
in the centre of the ceiling. The effect is dingy with shadows all
around.*

TERRY   Billeting Officer's been in the house.
ROSIE   How do you know?
TERRY   The electricity. Mr Forbes wouldn't have left it on
  when he went off to the war.

They go through the door and down the steps into the room.

BEN   Pongs a bit.

ROSIE   They'll see the light from outside.

TERRY   There's no window. Just that little grill thing in the corner.

BEN   Junk. This is where he dumps everything he doesn't want.

ROSIE   Old furniture.

BEN   Papers.

ROSIE   One big rubbish bin.

TERRY   In wartime, though, the best place in the house.

BEN   Eh?

TERRY   It's a shelter, see? Thick walls. Stone. Look at those beams up there. They won't ever collapse. And something else... *He moves a small cupboard* ...a sink. And running water. You could live down here. Safe from the bombs. And the enemy.

ROSIE   Enemy?

Terry goes up to the door.

TERRY   It's a big, thick door. Watch. *He locks it with the key* You can lock it from inside. Nobody can get us. We're safe.

BEN   *uneasy* Who would want to get us?

TERRY   The Germans. They'd have to shoot through the lock, though.

Pause

ROSIE   Better leave it open for now.

Terry *unlocks the door.*

TERRY   Don't you see? We could use this room, make it our space.

BEN   Yeah. Like a headquarters.

TERRY   Mr Forbes won't mind. He knows about war. We'd look after all his things.

ROSIE   Hey, look what I've found. Letters. ***Rosie has opened a box containing letters in bundles*** They're all from here. Look, Allsprings House on the front. He has special envelopes. *She opens one* It's written by him. See, his signature, Forbes-Lomax.

She reads.

BEN   Same address on all of them.

ROSIE   To a lady.

TERRY   *with instant fury* Put 'em away.

ROSIE   Shut up. I want to read them.

TERRY   I said, put 'em away. They're his letters. You're not to touch them.

ROSIE   They'll tell us something about him. I want to know. Anyway, you're not telling me what to do.

She picks up a bundle in defiance. **Terry** *snatches them and they spill everywhere.*

TERRY   See what you've done.

ROSIE   You did that.

BEN   Better put them back in the box, Rosie.

ROSIE   I don't get you, Terry. You don't mind sneaking into his house, but you go mad about us reading his letters.

TERRY   He's a soldier fighting in the war. We should look after his house, not mess it around. Protect it for him.

ROSIE   How's he to know I've read his letters?

TERRY   *with steely determination* They're private.

Rosie *decides it's not worth the battle and puts the letters back into the box.*

TERRY   In wartime, you've got to have a leader. This room is a good place for us. I found it, so I should be leader. *He looks at* **Ben** Ben?

Ben *nods.* **Terry** *looks at* **Rosie.**

ROSIE   We don't need a leader.

TERRY   We do.

ROSIE   Why?

TERRY   This is a special place. The war has brought us here. Somebody has to be in charge...make decisions...or it'll be spoilt.

ROSIE   What decisions?

TERRY   *glaring at her* Somebody has to be leader.

ROSIE   What for?

TERRY   I've told you.

ROSIE   Oh, have it your way. I don't mind.

Pause.

TERRY   Right, the first thing we have to do, is swear to keep this room secret. And how we got in.

ROSIE Who's there to tell?

TERRY The other evacuees when they come.

ROSIE How are you going to keep it secret from them?

TERRY I've got the key. We'll sneak in without 'em seeing.

BEN That'll make it a better secret. Them not knowing we're in here.

TERRY Ben? You swear?

Ben looks at Rosie, then back at Terry.

BEN OK, I swear.

TERRY *to Rosie* You?

ROSIE I'll swear if I can take a bundle of those letters to read.

TERRY No letters. Swear.

ROSIE No.

TERRY Swear.

ROSIE I might, I might not.

TERRY You heard me.

ROSIE What does it matter? If it makes you happy, I swear.

Terry relaxes a little.

TERRY To make this room a base, we'll have to sort things. This stuff here into that corner, and clear round the sink. *To Ben* Well...get started.

Terry and Ben set to work. Rosie sits on a box and watches them, now looking more like an outsider.

Music. The voice of Winston Churchill fades in.

CHURCHILL '...the Battle of Britain is about to begin. Upon this battle depends the survival of Christian civilisation. Upon it depends our own British life and the long continuity of our institutions and our Empire. Though all the fury and might of the enemy must very soon be turned upon us, Hitler knows that he will have to break this island or lose the war. If we stand up to him, all Europe may be free and the life of the world may move forward into a broad sunlit upland...'

Music increases, then fades.

SCENE SEVEN

The front garden of Peggy's House. A sunny day. Bedsheets are hanging on the line at the rear to dry. **Liam** *is sitting in a deck chair supervising 'Digging for Victory' work with* **Rosie, Ben** *and* **Terry.** *He is a slim and quite handsome figure, and speaks with a light Irish accent.*

LIAM Now we want the rows good and straight with the soil well turned over. Potatoes in the first row, runner beans behind. You've got it. Maybe we'll have some carrots too, eh? Pity about the flowers, but it's all in a good cause. You're doing fine. I'd be with you there myself, but I have to rest up a while.

BEN I'm puffed.

LIAM The more we plant, the more we shall have to eat. Stick with it a little longer there Benny. You're in the army, see? The land army. All over the country, the parks and gardens, lawns and borders are being turned over so we can grow more food. This way, Hitler will never starve us out. That's how they used to do it, you know, in the old days. Surround the enemy, keep 'em penned in, and wait. Sooner or later, starvation would drive 'em to surrender. Well, it won't work with us, because we're digging for victory.

TERRY *throwing his spade down* This is stupid, I'm not doing any more.

LIAM No place for slackers now, Terry.

ROSIE Can we have a rest in a minute, Uncle Liam?

LIAM Ah well, why not? Save the energy of the troops. I bet you're thirsty too, eh? Thought you would be. So here.

From his chair **Liam** *uses a stick to lift a tea towel off some drinks on a tray. They each take one.*

BEN What was it like at Dunkirk, Uncle Liam?

LIAM Well, I did a few hours sunbathing. Bit noisy at the time, mind. Nice beaches, though. All in all, I'd stick to Blackpool if I were you.

TERRY Did the German planes machine-gun you?

LIAM They did too. Quite hot it was for us there.

BEN What were you doing on the beach?

LIAM Things weren't going too well for us in France. The Germans have a strong army, and they're on their own side of the water.

TERRY   Drove you back to the sea, didn't they?

LIAM   I guess they did just that, Terry. Sure you weren't there yourself? 'Tis true though, we were there on the beach, the Germans coming up behind with their tanks and planes, and nothing in front of us but the sea. Sitting ducks with nowhere to hide but a sand castle. I thought of swimming for it, then I thought better of the idea. So I didn't. And all the while, the Messerschmitts were coming down low. We took pot shots at 'em with the rifles, but they move pretty fast, you see? And then, would you believe it, a miracle happened. First one boat, then another, and soon lots and lots of boats coming over the horizon across the water to rescue us. I tell you, every little tub with sails no bigger than a handkerchief was out there. What a sight! The sea was thick with 'em. I wouldn't have been surprised to see someone paddling a bath. When they got to the shore, they pulled our boys into the boats, gave 'em a welcome with a cup of tea, a sandwich and a blanket, and then headed for home. Sailing back was sweet. Most of us were dead tired. But every now and then you could hear a boat not far away strike up in song. *Pause* And that's how we said cheerio to the Hun and made it home.

TERRY   How did you get your wound?

LIAM   A bit of stray shrapnel as I was getting into the boat. Had to have a little bit of first aid on the way back, but I'm still living and breathing. I thank God for that.

Peggy comes out and starts working in the garden.

ROSIE   Does that mean that Hitler will come over here?

LIAM   Why should he do that?

ROSIE   We're the next country after France.

LIAM   He might, but he won't find it easy.

BEN   Why?

LIAM   He'd have to cross the English channel and we'd see him coming.

ROSIE   You did it.

LIAM   Eh?

ROSIE   Cross the channel. They couldn't stop the boats from Dunkirk.

LIAM   Well, if he decides to come he won't do it that way.

TERRY   He'd drop soldiers by parachute where they can't be seen.

LIAM   At night, in quiet places, where they'd lie low for a bit. First though, you'd have spies to find out the lie of the land, which communications to destroy, bridges to blow up, and the places where all the valuables are hidden.

BEN Who'd do that?

LIAM Fifth Columnists.

BEN What?

LIAM People who want Hitler to win the war.

ROSIE In England?

LIAM You can be sure of it. Some people like him. But you won't be able to spot 'em. You know why?

BEN Why?

LIAM Because the spy's trick is to look normal. Give nothing away. And all the while they're doing mischief.

TERRY There could be some round here, right now.

LIAM Maybe. Who knows? That's why we have to 'Keep It Under Your Hat'. 'Careless Talk Costs Lives'. Good advice. You never know who might be listening.

Pause

ROSIE If the Germans do come, will it be soon?

LIAM *changing his tone* Goodness, we're talking nonsense here, it's not going to happen at all.

Pause.

TERRY *with sudden urgency* We've got to go. You two, come with me.

ROSIE What?

TERRY Come with me. I'm telling you.

ROSIE I heard you.

TERRY It's important.

LIAM There's something buzzin' in the lad's head. Better go with him before he explodes.

***Ben** follows **Terry**, and then **Rosie** reluctantly follows. **Peggy** has been listening to **Liam** while doing the garden.*

PEGGY You'll frighten them, talking that way.

LIAM Not a bit of it. They love the talk. It's exciting.

SCENE EIGHT

The basement room in Allsprings House. **Rosie** *and* **Ben** *are sitting on boxes.* **Terry** *paces up and down, agitated.*

ROSIE   You're mad, you are, Terry.

TERRY   If the Germans come, they'll want to capture the cities. Big cities like Manchester. You can't land troops on buildings. You have to land 'em outside the city in places where they can plan an attack.

ROSIE   Like here, eh?

TERRY   Like here. Can't you see, it's perfect. Enough land for soldiers to drop by parachute. Trees to hide in. This house. They'll make it their base.

BEN   Here? Where we are now? *Pause* Nah, they wouldn't. Anyway, there's the army barracks on the other side.

TERRY   Don't be stupid. Only women train there. They won't be any use.

ROSIE   How are the Germans going to know about this place?

TERRY   Like he said – spies.

ROSIE   You mean somebody's watching us and sending messages to Hitler?

TERRY   You don't believe it, do you?

ROSIE   No, I don't.

TERRY   That's what Hitler wants you to think, you stupid fool, 'cause then he can take us by surprise. Can't you see? He' s got soldiers in France and now he's coming here.

BEN   Terry may be right, Rosie.

Rosie has no reply.

TERRY   Do you know the first thing they'll do if they capture this house?

BEN   What?

TERRY   Loot all the valuables.

BEN   Steal everything?

TERRY   Make money, see? Pay for guns and tanks.

BEN   I know what we could do.

TERRY   Go on.

BEN   We could hide all the valuable stuff in his room. There's only one key.

ROSIE   *to* **Ben** Now you're going soft in the head.

TERRY   No, he's not. Mr Forbes is a brave soldier fighting for us against Hitler. We can protect his house while he's away. Keep it safe for his return.

ROSIE   Locking it all in here won't make any difference. Like you said, the Germans could shoot the door down if they wanted to.

TERRY   The stuff will be safer in here. I'm leader and I say we do it.

ROSIE   Not with me you're not.

BEN   Rosie, it'll be better with you. The evacuees...

ROSIE   What?

BEN   We'll have to do it before the new evacuees come. Once they're here, we won't be able to get into the rooms up above. Help us do it.

TERRY   We'll have to stay hidden.

ROSIE   *with determination* I'm going home.

She makes a move to go.

TERRY   I'm giving an order. We all do it.

ROSIE   Get out of my way, Terry. Ben, you're coming with me.

BEN   Rosie!

ROSIE   I said you're coming with me.

Ben doesn't move.

ROSIE   You coming or not?

Pause.

BEN   No.

TERRY   He's following my orders, not yours.

ROSIE   Is he, then? Well, you'd better watch out, because if you get Ben into trouble, Terry, I'll make trouble for you. Now let me out.

Terry still blocks her way.

TERRY   You swore to keep this room secret.

ROSIE   Oh yeah.

TERRY   Swear again or I won't let you pass.

ROSIE   You're a little Hitler yourself, get out of my way!

TERRY   You heard.

He doesn't budge.

ROSIE   *very angry* Move, Terry!

TERRY   Swear!

ROSIE   *pulling at him* Let me out!

Terry raises an arm to strike back.

ROSIE   Don't you dare touch me.

Pause. She gives in.

ROSIE   All right, all right. I swear not to tell your precious secret. Now let me out.

Terry slowly steps to one side.

ROSIE   *at the door* Anyway, what about the Billeting Officer? She might be one of your spies. Anything missing and she'll know.

She goes out.

BEN   She may be right.
TERRY   We'll have to take chance on it. The Billeting Officer won't have been here much. We can hide some things and not others, so she won't notice. We can cover up.
BEN   Better get started. The evacuees may arrive anytime.
TERRY   We'll begin at the top of the house. She'd better keep her mouth shut, your sister. Or she'll be sorry.

They go out.

A low, menacing drone of massed planes in the distance. Pictures of the first big air raid on London and the sound of fires burning. A radio broadcast fades in.

BBC COMMENTATOR   '...As I walked along the streets, it was almost impossible to believe that these fires could be subdued. I was walking between solid walls of fire. Roofs of shops and office buildings came down with a roaring crash. Panes of glass were cracking everywhere with the heat and every street was criss-crossed with innumerable lengths of hose. Men were fighting the fires from the top of hundred foot ladders, others were pushing their way into buildings taking the jet to the core of the fire...'

SCENE NINE

*The kitchen in Peggy's House. **Liam** is at the table with ration books, working out coupons for the shopping. **Peggy** is cleaning and polishing. She looks at a photograph of her husband **Danny** on the mantelpiece.*

LIAM   London must be a living hell. Did we think we'd ever live to see the day, eh? Hundreds killed. Innocents all. Burnt alive in their beds. That evil, murderous Hitler. It was a dark day for the world when he was born, but he'll taste the everlasting fires himself one day, if there's any justice at all. *He turns the pages of a ration book* Oh, Heavens, how many coupons is it for sugar?

Peggy is absorbed in her work.

LIAM   20 points a month for jam, biscuits and what else. How can any mortal live on that? *He writes out a shopping list* This is just the beginning. Now the enemy has got the idea, those planes will be over, night after night. There are guns all round London, anti-aircraft, but they can't be much use. The planes fly too high. Still, the noise of the guns going off make people feel a lot better. *Pause – he looks at Peggy* He's on your mind again, isn't he? Your husband. No letter still.

PEGGY   Does it show that much?

LIAM   Well, every time you worry about him, you do the housework, and the more you worry, the harder you work.

PEGGY   I suppose I do.

Angie enters.

ANGIE   You've heard the news about London? Over 400 planes they reckon. This is just the beginning, they'll be after the other cities next. Well, one thing it's done is to sort out what I have to do. They're putting an ack-ack battery in the field next to Allsprings House. I'll do my special training here.

PEGGY   What do they need guns here for?

ANGIE   Bombers heading for Manchester are likely to come over this way.

PEGGY   German bombers over here?

ANGIE   It's only a matter of time before they attack cities in the north. They'll bring the war to everybody.

LIAM   We'll need air raid shelters.

PEGGY   What shall we tell the children?

ANGIE   The truth.

PEGGY   About families being blown to bits and burnt alive?

LIAM   No point in raising unnecessary fears.

PEGGY   *pointedly* That's fine, coming from you.

LIAM   Keep the children's mind off the business while we can.

ANGIE   They'll worry more if they are not told the truth.

PEGGY   How much truth do they need to know? They came here to get away from the bombs.

ANGIE   Peggy, you're not facing up to reality.

PEGGY   Here we go again. Look, I've got to be off to work in a minute. Popeye's calling and you know how I don't like to disappoint him.

She goes out.

Liam stares at Angie affectionately.

ANGIE   *aware of his gaze* What are you looking at?

LIAM   You.

ANGIE   Liam!

LIAM   Has anybody said how fine you look in that uniform.

ANGIE   Liam, please, not in the house.

LIAM   How about out of the house?

ANGIE   No! A minute ago you were talking about bombs.

LIAM   I know.

ANGIE   And now you are making a pass at me.

LIAM   Terrible, isn't it? But I blame the war. It causes decay of all moral scruples.

He sings 'A Nightingale Sang In Berkeley Square'.

LIAM   'That certain night, the night we met, there was magic abroad in the air...'

Rosie enters looking downcast. Angie glares at Liam.

LIAM   OK, OK, I promise. No more. *To Rosie* The boys deserted you, eh?

ROSIE   No, I've deserted them.

LIAM   There's a letter there from your mum.

Rosie brightens and sits at the table to read the letter. Peggy re-enters with her coat.

PEGGY   *to Liam* The boys are spending a lot of time over at Allsprings.

LIAM   Playing soldiers in the gardens, that's all.

PEGGY   I think Terry's a bit beyond playing soldiers.

LIAM   You're telling me to keep an eye on things, eh?

Peggy sees he has got the point and goes out. Liam looks at Rosie.

LIAM   Your mum all right?
ROSIE   Yes. She misses us.

Pause.

LIAM   Do you know how many coupons for sugar?

SCENE TEN

The basement room in Allsprings House. **Terry** *and* **Ben** *have collected paintings, vases, small statues, swords, etc.*

BEN   *exhausted* How much more Terry?
TERRY   There's plenty more space, yet. We keep going.
BEN   It's heavy, this stuff.
TERRY   Time's against us. Once the evacuees arrive, we have to go into hiding.
BEN   I've got to have a rest.

Ben sits down.

TERRY   She could be right about the Billeting Officer.
BEN   Eh?
TERRY   Being a spy. She's just the sort of person who could be a spy.
BEN   How can you tell?
TERRY   Who'd suspect her? She knows the area, talks to everybody, collects information. It's her job to watch this house. *Pause* She'll never find us though. Once we've got all this stuff safe.
BEN   What?
TERRY   You've got to be like a spy. See what I've got. *He takes a telescope and a pair of binoculars out of a box* For watching people. You have to keep in the shadows, hidden. If there is a spy around, we'll soon find out. They'll leave a clue by mistake.
BEN   Can I have one?
TERRY   The telescope's yours.

Ben takes the telescope and tries it.

BEN   *puzzled* Terry, is this a game or is it real?
TERRY   Grow up, Ben.

Terry walks around the room.

TERRY   We'll soon have it sorted. You know, you could live in here. Bed over there. Plenty of drawers and things. There's electricity so you could even have something to cook on.

Ben *is puzzled.*

BEN   Live here? *Pause* Who Terry?
TERRY   Anybody...after the war, you'll need places for people to live. Soldiers coming back.
BEN   I suppose so.

Pause.

TERRY   Like my dad. He could live in this room after the war.
BEN   What?
TERRY   When he comes back...he could stay here.
BEN   What about home? Wouldn't he want to go home?

Pause.

BEN   What about Mr Forbes?
TERRY   What about him?
BEN   Would he know? About your dad living here?
TERRY   Course he would.
BEN   But what'll your mum think?

Pause.

TERRY   He'd like it here. Him and Mr Forbes. Two soldiers, war heroes together. Yeah, my dad would be happy in this room. He wouldn't want one of those posh rooms upstairs. *Pause* They'd put their uniforms behind the glass with the others.

Ben *looks at* ***Terry,*** *trying to understand.*

BEN   What does your dad do? In the army?
TERRY   I told you. He's a sniper. An expert. He can stay hidden in one place for days, just waiting, then at the right moment – bang.
BEN   Go on.
TERRY   What I'm telling you is a secret between you and me. Not a word to your sister. I don't trust her.
BEN   No, Terry. *Pause* Terry.
TERRY   What?
BEN   Where will you go after the war?
TERRY   Stay here with him. Probably. We're guarding this

stuff for everybody. Keeping it safe. We may have to sleep here ourselves to be sure it stays secret.

BEN   Sleep here. During the night?

TERRY   *suddenly alert* Somebody's outside.

They listen.

BEN   I can't hear anything.

TERRY   Could be the Billeting Officer. She won't ever find the place where we got in. I'm too clever for that. *He listens* Gone.

BEN   You wouldn't have us stay here during the night, would you?

TERRY   Just make sure your sister keeps her mouth shut. Now, we need more stuff.

BEN   Terry, I can't carry any more.

TERRY   Get moving.

Ben gets up wearily. Terry goes out, Ben follows.
Music.

SCENE ELEVEN

*The kitchen in Peggy's House. It is evening. **Peggy** enters from work. She looks on the mantelpiece for a letter from her husband, but is disappointed. She smells something cooking, goes over to the oven, and opens it. She looks puzzled, then closes the door and goes out. After a few moments, **Liam** enters, goes to the oven, opens it and looks pleased with himself.*

*Lights cross-fade to the bedroom where **Terry** is at the window keeping watch on Allsprings House through his binoculars. **Ben** is reading his mother's letter. **Rosie** is sitting on her bed watching **Ben.***

BEN   She'll be back soon.

ROSIE   I don't think she likes being here, away from home.

BEN   *keeping his voice low* Rosie...

ROSIE   Don't worry, she will come.

BEN   I know that.

ROSIE   Feeling homesick?

BEN   No, it's not that. *In a whisper* The room in the house, you won't tell about it, will you?

ROSIE   *also in whisper* You're not getting yourself into trouble, are you, Ben?

BEN   No, no.

TERRY   What are you two whispering about? Eh?

ROSIE   It's nothing to do with you, Terry.

TERRY   Something in it, isn't there? If you've told her anything...

ROSIE   Well, what then...

Pause.

TERRY   Somebody could get hurt.

ROSIE   Look here, Terry, you lay a finger on anybody and I'll tell everything.

Liam is heard coming upstairs singing an entry fanfare. Terry hides the binoculars. Liam enters with something under a fancy looking dish. With a flourish he lifts off the lid to reveal a cake. Ben and Rosie look delighted. Terry shows little reaction.

LIAM   Chef's special. Make the most of it, there won't be much chance in future because of the rationing. *He cuts it up and gives Rosie and Ben a slice each* Are you having some, Terry, me boy?

TERRY   Yeah.

Liam gives Terry a piece. Terry eats it looking rather awkward.

BEN   It's good.

ROSIE   Thanks. *Pause* Will the bombers come to Manchester, Uncle Liam?

LIAM   Here's me trying to create a little diversion, but you kids are too smart.

ROSIE   They may want to bomb the factory where my dad works.

LIAM   Let 'em try, that's what I say. The Royal Air Force will give 'em hell. One of ours is worth three of theirs, I tell you. They've proved it. Mr Hitler will think twice before he sends his planes over to Manchester, because he knows full well it'll be like putting 'em up as target practice for our boys. *Pause* You liking the cake, Terry?

TERRY   Yeah.

LIAM   You've been spending a lot of time at the house over there recently. Good fun, is it?

Terry *glares at **Ben** and **Rosie**.*

BEN   Some new evacuees are coming to stay there.

LIAM   Evacuees, in that fancy place? What are you getting up to now, got something good going there, eh? *Silence from all three* I know, state secrets, and I'm spying. Listen, kids, there's something I need a hand with tomorrow, so I'm asking you to report for duty at nine hundred hours in the front garden.

BEN   What for?

LIAM   You'll see.

Terry goes out.

LIAM   Where you off to, Terry me lad?

TERRY   *from outside* The lav.

LIAM   Right, in the garden in the morning. *Nods from **Ben** and **Rosie*** Good night now, and say a prayer for your mum.

He goes out.

ROSIE   Ben, give me the letter.

BEN   You won't say anything to Uncle Liam.

ROSIE   About Terry? I'm not scared of him.

BEN   He thinks you're going to blab the secret.

ROSIE   I know he does.

Terry *returns. **Ben** looks guilty. **Rosie** slips the letter under the blanket.*

TERRY   There is something in that letter, I can tell.

ROSIE   I've told you, there isn't. Read it if you like. Here.

*She hands **Terry** the letter. **Terry** does not take it.*

ROSIE   Go on. Read it. *Pause* You can read, can't you, Terry?

Terry *turns away. He takes the binoculars and looks out of the window to Allsprings. **Rosie** watches him.*

ROSIE   Terry, it's dark.

SCENE TWELVE

*The front garden of Peggy's house. **Liam** is digging a hole for an air-raid shelter. **Rosie** and **Ben** are helping. **Terry** is there but not involved.*

ROSIE   Why do you have to put an air-raid shelter in a hole?

LIAM   Well, if it's standing out of the ground, the blast of a bomb would blow it over. Then you'd be rattling around inside.

BEN   If a bomb dropped right on it, would you be safe?

LIAM   No, you'd cop it. But, if the house collapsed on top of the shelter, you'd be all right then. May take a while to dig you out, but you'd be alive. That's why you must have a kettle in there with you for a cup of tea. Terry, you should be over here working. *Terry does not respond* In a world of his own, that lad.

The three carry on digging.

ROSIE   Are you feeling better now, Uncle Liam?

LIAM   Well, I couldn't be doing this a week ago. So something's mending. All the worse for me, though. The sooner I'm fit, the sooner I'm back in the army.

*Gloria Dawkins and **Margaret** enter and stand a few yards away. They are waiting for somebody. **Gloria** is attractive and well dressed, and speaks with a London accent. **Margaret** looks very like **Rosie**. **Gloria** watches **Liam**, and **Liam**, aware of her gaze, digs a little faster. Gloria smiles.*

LIAM   Hi, there.

GLORIA   What are you digging? A bomb crater?

LIAM   That's right, we'd like to have our very own in the front garden. To be one up on the neighbours, see?

GLORIA   Got the army on shelter duty, have they?

LIAM   Ah! The uniform. That's right. The rest of the platoon are sorting out around the back.

*Rosie is looking at **Margaret**, wondering who she is.*

GLORIA   I thought I was coming up here to get away from this sort of thing.

LIAM   Where you from then?

GLORIA   London.

LIAM   So you know all about bombs and destruction.

GLORIA   Just a bit. This is my niece, Margaret. *Puts her arm around **Margaret's** shoulder* She's been having a bad time of it, so we're getting her out for a while.

LIAM   Grim down there, eh?

GLORIA   It's every night now. The raids are getting bigger and bigger.

LIAM   Diabolical murderers.

GLORIA   What's the army doing south of Manchester, anyway?

LIAM   Here for just a short while. I got caught up in the Dunkirk business. Doctor's orders.

GLORIA   You know what the rough stuff's like too.

LIAM   *turning to **Margaret*** Well, Margaret, you should meet our Rosie. Make friends. You'd like that, eh, Rosie?

Rosie nods. The two girls are clearly pleased to meet each other.

LIAM   Oh, and this is Ben, Rosie's brother. They're from Manchester. Evacuees, like yourselves. And that's Terry, another evacuee. *To the girls* Well, don't be bashful the two of you. Rosie, ask Margaret if she would like a drink. She's had a long journey.

ROSIE   *to **Margaret*** Would you like one?

MARGARET   Yes.

ROSIE   You can come inside if you like. See where we are staying.

Terry looks concerned about this new friendship.

ROSIE   Can I take Margaret in the house, Uncle Liam?

LIAM   Of course you can. There's a bottle of Tizer in the kitchen.

*The two girls go off into the house. **Terry** follows them anxiously but not so as to attract their attention. During the next part of the scene **Rosie** and **Margaret** can be seen making friends. **Terry** spies on them.*

GLORIA   Thank you.

LIAM   What for?

GLORIA   Helping to get them started.

LIAM   You can see they'll hit it off.

GLORIA   Poor little Margaret had a nasty experience that's given her nightmares ever since. *Pause* Where's that Billeting Officer? 10.30 she said.

LIAM   You'll be glad to get out of London yourself, then.

GLORIA   Couldn't have worked better. It's my job, see? Been sent up here to my boss's place. Over there, Allsprings House.

LIAM   I see.

GLORIA   I work at the Albery Hotel, Kensington, near the Albert Hall. My boss left instructions, see. If the bombing got bad, the residents could take themselves off to his house up in the country. They're long stay residents. In their seventies, most of them.

Hearing this, **Ben** *becomes alert.* **Gloria** *looks at her watch.*

GLORIA   I wonder if I got the time wrong?

LIAM   So you're the advance party to do the spit and polish before they arrive.

GLORIA   That's right.

LIAM   Generous fella, your Mr Forbes-Lomax.

GLORIA   You know him then.

LIAM   I can't say we have met.

The **A.R.P. Warden** *enters.*

A.R.P. WARDEN   Number 6. Any of you the owner or resident here?

LIAM   I am. Resident, that is.

A.R.P. WARDEN   My records say two people, is this correct?

LIAM   Two people what?

A.R.P. WARDEN   Currently resident in this house.

LIAM   Wrong. Six.

A.R.P. WARDEN   Evacuees?

LIAM   Three evacuees and me makes four.

A.R.P. WARDEN   It is my duty, you see, to ensure that everybody in the area has adequate shelter accommodation...

LIAM   That's good.

A.R.P. WARDEN   ...and that procedures in the event of a raid are fully understood.

LIAM   Well, there's a shelter here going up before your very eyes. For six people, when completed. How about that?

A.R.P. WARDEN   *making a note on his clipboard*
Shel-ter-for-six-at-num-ber-six.

GLORIA   They have a soldier here to build their shelter for them.

34

A.R.P. WARDEN   All assistance is, of course, welcome.

GLORIA   And he's had one distraction after another this morning. At the rate he's going, the war will be finished before the shelter.

A.R.P. WARDEN   A warning siren has been installed approximately one hundred yards down the road. In the event of a raid, you should turn off electricity and gas, and proceed in an orderly fashion to the shelter.

GLORIA   What about the evacuees in the big house?

A.R.P. WARDEN   Eh? What evacuees? News to me...that Billeting Officer...how many?

GLORIA   Maybe 10 or 12.

A.R.P. WARDEN   There's no shelter in the grounds. They'll have to use the street shelter near the town centre.

GLORIA   So when the siren goes off we have to run for it.

A.R.P. WARDEN   Looks like it.

GLORIA   The evacuees are all over 70.

A.R.P. WARDEN   Ah...

*The **Billeting Officer** enters.*

BILLETING OFFICER   Miss Dawkins?

GLORIA   That's me.

A.R.P. WARDEN   Well, I'll be on my way. Remember to practise your air raid drill at regular intervals, and to keep a tight blackout at all times.

*The **A.R.P. Warden** leaves.*

BILLETING OFFICER   Sorry I'm late.

GLORIA   Don't worry. We have been entertained.

BILLETING OFFICER   I have the keys here. Shall we go over to the house?

LIAM   Nice to meet you, Miss Dawkins.

GLORIA   Gloria.

LIAM   Gloria. I'm Liam.

GLORIA   And you...Liam.

*Pause. **Rosie** and **Margaret** come out of the house followed by **Terry**, looking very agitated.*

LIAM   Hey, you lot, your new evacuees are going to be a bunch of old fogies. *Laughing* What do you think o' that?

***Rosie** and **Margaret** laugh. **Ben** looks at **Terry** who is more concerned about the girls.*

GLORIA   Would Rosie like to come over with Margaret?
ROSIE   Yes, please.
LIAM   A fine idea.
GLORIA   Right then, Rosie. Let's go.

The three go off with the **Billeting Officer.** *Liam watches* ***Gloria***.

LIAM   *to* **Ben** *and* **Terry** Enough digging for today. Finish off tomorrow.

Liam *goes into the house.* **Terry** *comes forward with a fixed look towards Allsprings.*

BEN   What about the stuff, Terry? Suppose they notice?
TERRY   That's how they do it, see?
BEN   What?
TERRY   Spies.
BEN   What do you mean?
TERRY   It's a cover. Got to be. The girl.
BEN   Terry, the stuff. They'll know it's missing.
TERRY   They don't know what's there. They'll think Mr Forbes has stored it somewhere while the war's on.
BEN   What if they find out?
TERRY   They won't. Not unless your sister blabs.
BEN   She won't, Terry.
TERRY   She can't get in there anyway. *He holds up the key to the basement room* If she tells...

Lights fade down to a spot on **Terry.** *The menacing drone of planes returns.*

SCENE THIRTEEN

The basement room in Allsprings House. Towards the end of the interval, **Terry** *and* **Ben** *are seen organising the valuables in the basement room. They have arranged a small living space with access to the sink. When the lights come up they sit down and survey their work.*

BEN   They must have heard us.
TERRY   Nah! Thick walls, these are.
BEN   Through the ceiling.
TERRY   There's a stone floor on top.

BEN   Maybe they saw us coming in.

TERRY   It's better they see us in the gardens. Get used to us there. When we go into the house, they'll think we're somewhere in the trees. *Pause* As long as your sister keeps her mouth shut. *Pause* It's good practice, anyway.

BEN   What do you mean?

TERRY   Living in secret. Right underneath. Best place. Under their noses. It's what snipers do. *Pause* All we need now is a bed.

BEN   What for?

TERRY   Sleeping in, stupid.

BEN   We can't take a bed.

TERRY   And some plates and things. Then we'll have everything.

BEN   I'm not sleeping here.

TERRY   It's not for you.

BEN   The beds are too heavy. We'll never lift one.

TERRY   A mattress then. Some pillows.

BEN   I'm not taking anything more.

TERRY   You've got no choice.

BEN   What do you mean?

TERRY   I give the orders.

Ben has no reply.

TERRY   Where's the telescope?

BEN   Here somewhere.

TERRY   From now on we keep an eye on your sister and the new girl.

Lights fade. Radio.

BBC ANNOUNCER   'Here is the midnight news and this is Alvar Lidel reading it. Up to 10 o'clock 175 planes have been destroyed in today's raids over this country. Today was the most costly for the German airforce for nearly a month. In daylight raids, between 350 and 400 enemy aircraft were launched in 2 attacks against London and South East England. About half of them were shot down.'

SCENE FOURTEEN

*Peggy's House. Outside the house, the Anderson shelter in the front garden has been completed. Inside the house, **Angie** is up a ladder putting up blackout curtains with help from **Liam**. The room is strewn with pieces of blackout material.*

LIAM   A tight blackout, the warden said. You leave a chink of light showing and he'll bawl at you.

ANGIE   He likes it. Makes him feel important.

LIAM   No harm, I suppose. Just doing his little bit. *Pause* So what's the news from the Barracks?

ANGIE   The ack-ack guns are here and in place. They're setting up the searchlights tomorrow. That'll be my job. Searchlight operator. Someone's coming up from London to train us.

LIAM   Serious business, then?

ANGIE   Can you pass me the other curtain?

Liam does so.

ANGIE   The Germans aren't going to stop at London. They're going to hit the other big cities – Birmingham, Manchester etc. – anytime now. That's why there's a big rush on to get the defences in place.

LIAM   We're some way from the city here.

ANGIE   That's the whole point. Shoot the planes down before they get there.

Pause

LIAM   Important job, searchlight operator. You'll need a cool head and a steady hand for it. *He watches her* But I guess that's you, eh? There'll be no chinks coming through that curtain. I can tell without the light on.

ANGIE   It's exciting. The Barracks are buzzing. Everybody is itching to get into the action. The raids on London have done it. Shouldn't say it, I know, but we want revenge. Hit the enemy where it hurts.

LIAM   Beats selling buttons. *Pause* I hope you're not messing up Forbes's estate. With the guns, and that.

ANGIE   Oh yes, I forgot. News came through. He's in North Africa, in charge of a tank regiment. They reckon that's where the next big push is going to be. A war in the desert.

LIAM   So he'll not be too concerned about his flower borders at the moment, eh?

ANGIE   Mr Forbes-Lomax is having the time of his life.

LIAM   How do you know that?

ANGIE   The war's his heaven sent opportunity to follow
the great Forbes-Lomax family tradition in war.

LIAM   What's that?

ANGIE   Either die or return smothered in glory.

LIAM   Well then, I guess he'd be quite happy with you
shooting down German planes from his field.

Angie looks at Liam from the ladder.

LIAM   You'll do a fine job. Mind you, a pretty face like
yours could distract the attention of the gunners. Had you
thought about that?

ANGIE   *glaring at Liam* You promised.

Peggy enters from work.

PEGGY   Look at the state of the place.

ANGIE   We're nearly finished.

PEGGY   Keeping the house tidy these days is impossible. I
might as well give up.

*She goes over to the mantelpiece, looking for a letter, but
nothing has arrived. **Angie** and **Liam** watch her. She goes
out.*

LIAM   No letter yet?

ANGIE   I don't know what to say to her any more. She
thinks I don't understand.

LIAM   Well, everything she wanted has been taken away.

ANGIE   Her Danny boy.

LIAM   *sings quietly* 'Oh, Danny boy, the pipes, the pipes
are calling...' You'd think a letter would have got through by
now. The army has a postal service. Even in battle.

ANGIE   I don't think the post is the problem.

LIAM   Eh?

ANGIE   Some men don't like a house that's too neat and
tidy. Everything perfect. Nothing out of place.

LIAM   But they get married all the same. Is that it?

ANGIE   Yes, even though in their hearts, they want a wild
adventure.

LIAM   I see.

ANGIE   But they may not know that till they're away from home for a while. *Deliberately redirecting the conversation* Finished. Shall we ask for an inspection by the Warden?

Angie comes down the ladder but loses her balance as she turns on the last step. Liam catches her and for a moment holds her in his arms.

LIAM   Not me, this time.

Angie sees the funny side of the situation and laughs. Peggy enters and sees them.

PEGGY   Not that as well.

She sits at the table, puts her head into her hands and begins to weep. Angie comes over to comfort her.

ANGIE   Peggy, the more you hope, the worse it is each day. Best not to hope too much.
PEGGY   It's the only thing that keeps me going.
ANGIE   The house...you worry about it, and spend energy on housework you can't afford.
PEGGY   But it must be right for him when he comes back. As long as I'm hoping...can't you see, I have to do it.
ANGIE   Peggy, the war may go on for years. We must face that. If you're hoping to pick things up where they left off...
PEGGY   It's easy for you to talk, you're not married, or engaged even. You don't know what it's like. I'm not you, I don't like complications.

Rosie enters with Margaret.

LIAM   Hello again Margaret. Settled in across there?
MARGARET   Yes.
ANGIE   Hello.

Peggy is too preoccupied to take much notice.

ROSIE   I was wondering if Margaret could stay to tea.

A moment's silence, broken by Liam.

LIAM   Well, that's a fine idea. I myself will act as chef for the occasion. Come with me.

The three go out together. Peggy and Angie look at each other.

PEGGY   You're not starting anything with Liam, are you?
ANGIE   Peggy, I have more important things on my mind at the moment. Like getting back to the Barracks on time. I'm off.

40

PEGGY   It's good that Rosie has found a friend.
ANGIE   Yes.
PEGGY   I hope he's keeping an eye on the two boys.
ANGIE   Bye.

She goes out.

PEGGY   Bye.

SCENE FIFTEEN

The grounds of Allsprings House. **Terry** *and* **Ben** *are peering out from the shrubbery with the binoculars and telescope.* **Terry** *is watching Peggy's house,* **Ben** *is watching the new anti-aircraft guns.*

TERRY   They've gone inside.
BEN   See those guns?
TERRY   That new girl's a cover.
BEN   Ack-ack. They must be.
TERRY   If your sister let's the secret out...
BEN   Suppose they try to bomb these guns first?
TERRY   ...and makes her friend promise to say nothing...
BEN   They could though, couldn't they?
TERRY   What?
BEN   Bomb here first.
TERRY   We'd be safe.
BEN   Eh?
TERRY   The room. Perfect shelter. Everything sorted. All we need now is a store of food.
BEN   Food?
TERRY   Then we can go into hiding. *Pause* What are they doing in there? No way of knowing from here. *Pause* Ben, go after them.
BEN   What for?
TERRY   Find out if your sister's said anything.
BEN   I'm not spying on them.
TERRY   You heard me.
BEN   No.
TERRY   Get moving.
BEN   I said, no.
TERRY   I'm not going to tell you again.
BEN   You can't make me spy on my own sister.
TERRY   Can't I? Come here.

BEN   You're mad, you are. I've had enough of you.
TERRY   I said, come here.
BEN   No!
TERRY   Come here.

Ben turns towards Terry. Terry moves to him in a face to face confrontation.

TERRY   *with menace* Do it.
BEN   You can't make me.
TERRY   Do it!
BEN   No.

With sudden fury, Terry gives Ben a hard punch in the stomach. Ben doubles up and is badly winded.

BEN   *sobbing and trying to catch his breath* You...didn't... need...
TERRY   Don't you ever say 'no' to me. Do you hear?

SCENE SIXTEEN

The kitchen in Peggy's house. Peggy is still at the table in depressed mood after her words with Angie. Liam enters with a cabbage in each hand.

PEGGY   They grew quickly.
LIAM   I 'liberated' them from a field over the fence.
PEGGY   'Pinch For Victory'?
LIAM   Not quite. Call it living by your wits. Soldiers have to do it. Part of their training, see?
PEGGY   Where are the girls?
LIAM   Off to the shops with the ration books to get some things for tea.

Liam starts to prepare the meal.

LIAM   Is this the real Peggy I see before me?
PEGGY   What?
LIAM   You're not doing housework. The first time I've seen you sitting down.

Pause

PEGGY   Angie's right about me. Funny how we are so different. This war's the making of her, it's destroying me.

LIAM   Hold on, there.

PEGGY   It's true what she says. I just live for my husband.

LIAM   What's so bad about that?

PEGGY   When he's not here, there doesn't seem to be any point to anything. That makes me feel stupid.

LIAM   You're doing just fine. Why be so hard on yourself?

PEGGY   What's fine about pulling a drill handle 10,000 times a day? A monkey could do it.

LIAM   Still important work.

PEGGY   War work. War effort. Drudgery, that's what it is. *Pause* Why hasn't a letter come through?

LIAM   Don't go blaming yourself. The war does it to you. Makes you feel helpless, like you're worth nothing. Look here, Hitler's rampaging around Europe and I'm here peeling vegetables. *Brandishes a cabbage* And they're not even my own. We're not in control.

PEGGY   Angie is. You are. The war means something to you. You've answered the call. Noble patriots, both of you. Me, I just want it to stop and everything to carry on as it was before.

LIAM   Noble, am I? Well, how about that?

PEGGY   A 'Noble Hero of Dunkirk'.

LIAM   *in a more serious tone* Peggy, I cannot lie to you. Dunkirk was an unholy mess. Noble Heroes? When we saw the German army coming we turned round double smart and ran like the devil to save our lives. A disorderly mob, we were. Couldn't get out fast enough. Our orders were to destroy everything – guns, tanks, anything the enemy might pick up and use. *Pause* On the beach there were thousands of us, sitting targets for the German planes. All along, men dug in, bodies sprawling. It was like a slaughterhouse on a hot day. *Pause* Then the boats came. I thought right, this is it. I get out of my hole, make my way to the water. I'm going down the beach and one of the 'bodies' in the sand calls to me for help. In all the noise of the boats and the water, I heard him, calling to me in barely a whisper. Lying there he was, shot to pieces, his eyes looking straight at me, pleading. It was hopeless, I knew it. He would have died before we got him to the boat. *Pause* Now, if I'd have been noble as you call it, I'd have stayed there with him, told him the lads were coming for him any minute, and talked him to sleep with a story or two about what we'd do when we got back home. But no,

I'm looking at him and my head's telling me one living soldier is better than two dead ones. Save yourself. So I did, and for my sins I caught a piece of shrapnel in my stomach while I'm sitting on the deck of the boat. *Pause* So there's your noble Liam for you.

Pause.

PEGGY   You were right though, to save yourself.

LIAM   Maybe. But what for? More war? More fighting? Tomorrow I go for a medical check up. The result will be positive and I'll be back in the army. You know, I'd desert, only they shoot you for it.

Pause. He looks at **Peggy.**

LIAM   If you had some news, that would help, eh? A few scraps of information. Knowing nothing, that's the worst. It's bound to make you worry about him.

Peggy *nods.*

LIAM   You can't carry on the way you are. Something's got to change.

PEGGY   I know, but I don't know what.

LIAM   You don't have to follow orders like me. We can't stop the war, but we can do things to help us survive it.

PEGGY   Like what?

LIAM   Look, Peggy, change is happening already. Now's the time to do something. I've just been talking to Mrs Parks on the telephone. She's torn apart. When she's up there, she thinks she should be here, and when she's here, she wants to be home. The worry of it is making her ill. My guess is, when I go from here, she'll have the children back with her in Manchester.

PEGGY   I thought she was quite happy with the arrangement.

LIAM   Don't get me wrong. It's nothing to do with you or the house here. It's just that, in the end, separation's worse than bombs.

PEGGY   Leaving Terry here on his own? I'm not sure I fancy that.

LIAM   We could arrange another billet for him.

PEGGY   The Billeting Officer's been trying to find a place for ages.

LIAM   Some evacuees have gone home. There'll be places.

44

And that job, be honest, it's killing you. You don't have to do it. Find another one.

PEGGY   If I did that, it would be...well...unpatriotic.

LIAM   There's plenty of other work in the town. Good war effort stuff. I see they need someone at the Welfare Centre to distribute orange juice, cod liver oil and the like to mothers with babies. What could be better than that? Helping our young ones to be fit and healthy so that they can have a good life when this cruel war is over.

PEGGY   You may be right.

*Rosie and **Margaret** enter carrying shopping, followed by **Ben** concealing the telescope.*

ROSIE   Here are the things for tea, Uncle Liam.

PEGGY   *to Liam* I'll have a bath and think about it.

She goes out.

ROSIE   *angrily to **Ben*** You're up to something, Ben Parks. Following us, aren't you?

BEN   No.

ROSIE   Yes you are. You can't lie to me.

LIAM   Well done girls. You got everything on the list. Aha, the fizzy pop too. That'll be our champagne. Right, now to the rest of the preparations.

A knock on the door.

LIAM   See to that will you, Benny?

*Before **Ben** gets to the door, the **Billeting Officer** enters with urgency.*

BILLETING OFFICER   Is Peggy in?

LIAM   She's in the bath at the moment.

BILLETING OFFICER   I promised to bring her news of Terry's mother when it came through.

LIAM   Took a while, eh? But that's good. Tell me, if you like. I'll pass it on to Peggy.

*The **Billeting Officer** looks round at the children.*

LIAM   Right then, you lot. This is not for your ears. Make yourselves scarce for a while.

*Rosie and **Margaret** go out. **Ben** follows, but then sneaks back without being seen and hides behind the table. After a few moments the end of his telescope appears and fixes on the*

Billeting Officer's *face.*

LIAM   You've got a letter for Terry?

BILLETING OFFICER   No, and he won't be getting one.

LIAM   Why's that?

BILLETING OFFICER   I'd lock her up in Strangeways.

LIAM   Prison?

BILLETING OFFICER   No I wouldn't. Too good for the likes of her.

LIAM   You found her, then?

BILLETING OFFICER   The house. 36, Mostyn Street. But not his mum. And not a single stick of furniture in the place. All gone. Done a moonlight flit.

LIAM   Where to?

BILLETING OFFICER   Nobody knows. She's done it before apparently. That time, Terry went to stay with his gran, but she's dead now. A neighbour said she thought Terry's mum was planning something. Had a new fancy man in tow for a while. But she never let on where she was going.

LIAM   Saw her chance, eh?

BILLETING OFFICER   The evacuation was a perfect opportunity – a new life without Terry. Gone, she is, for good. They'll never find her. Not while the war's on.

LIAM   What about his dad?

BILLETING OFFICER   He went off before the war started and hasn't been seen since.

LIAM   The army?

BILLETING OFFICER   Could be. Anyway, it looks like we've got a better chance of getting hold of his dad than his mum. If we do, we'll ask him to get in touch. Something's got to be fixed up. If the war finishes next week, Terry's got nowhere to go. His mother's not going to appear like magic.

LIAM   It's an awful cruelty.

BILLETING OFFICER   I'd make a public example of her.

Pause.

LIAM   Well, thanks for coming round to tell us.

They walk to the door.

LIAM   Peggy is not in the best of spirits just now. News like this when you're trying to sort things out...well, I may wait a while before I tell her.

BILLETING OFFICER   But she needs to know.
LIAM   Leave that to me.

*They go out. **Ben** stands up from behind the table.*

SCENE SEVENTEEN

*Outside Peggy's House. **Rosie** and **Margaret** are sitting together. **Angie** is seen going into the house behind them.*

ROSIE   *offering **Margaret** a sweet* Have another one.
MARGARET   Thanks.
ROSIE   Lemon rock. My favourite. *Pause* Do you like it here?
MARGARET   Yes.
ROSIE   I thought you might be feeling homesick.
MARGARET   Why?
ROSIE   You often look like you're thinking things.
MARGARET   Do I?

*Pause. **Terry** appears but pretends not to notice them.*

MARGARET   Sometimes I have bad dreams.
ROSIE   What about?
MARGARET   I dream that our house has collapsed and they're trapped underneath. Nobody's come to help. I'm on my own trying to rescue them, but the bricks are too heavy.
ROSIE   I worry too. In case the bombers come to Manchester. At least we have an air-raid shelter. *Pause* What do you think of Allsprings House?
MARGARET   It's big and feels strange. I don't know if I'll get used to it.

*They notice **Terry**.*

ROSIE   Do you know about the man who lives there? The one in the picture in the hall.
MARGARET   Mr Forb...
ROSIE   Forbes-Lomax.
MARGARET   Only what my Aunt Gloria has told me.

Pause.

***Angie** enters.*

ANGIE   Tea's ready. A special one too. Your Uncle Liam makes a good housewife.

ROSIE   Tomorrow, let's go on a picnic. Just us two. *So that **Terry** can hear* Then we can talk without anybody overhearing.

*They go in. The focus shifts to **Terry** staring grimly towards Peggy's house. The low, distant drone of planes returns.*

SCENE EIGHTEEN

*The kitchen in Peggy's House. The table is laid out beautifully. **Liam**, **Peggy**, **Angie**, **Rosie**, **Margaret** and **Ben** sit down to eat.*

ROSIE   It looks lovely, Uncle Liam.

LIAM   A welcome tea for our new friend Margaret. Where's Terry?

BEN   Don't know.

LIAM   Better call him, Ben.

BEN   He won't come.

LIAM   Lying low, is he?

BEN   Don't know.

LIAM   He's got to eat sometime. Ah well, we'll not spoil the tea. He'll come in when he's hungry.

They begin to eat.

LIAM   How are you liking it, Margaret, over at Allsprings?

MARGARET   It's nice.

BEN   They've put guns and searchlights in the gardens.

LIAM   So they have, and guess who's going to be working them?

BEN   Angie?

LIAM   Chief searchlight operator. In charge of the whole battery, I'll bet, though she's too shy to admit it.

ROSIE   Why have they put the guns there?

ANGIE   To stop the planes getting through to Manchester...if they come this far.

ROSIE   The bombers still got through in London.

ANGIE   But anti-aircraft defences are getting better all the time. A good crew works like a team, the range finder plots the distance of the planes, then the searchlights...

PEGGY   Angie, you don't have to go into detail.

The table falls silent.

LIAM *looking towards **Angie*** It's the sneaky little fighter planes you need to watch out for.

PEGGY Liam!

LIAM No, it's true. A searchlight is a beautiful bright thing in the night sky. The planes fly like moths to a candle flame, straight down the beam, shooting all the way. If they put out the searchlights the guns are useless, see?

PEGGY Liam, will you please stop talking about bombs and killing. We may not get planes over Manchester.

A knock on the door.

ANGIE I'll go.

*Silence again at the table. **Angie** returns.*

ANGIE *To **Liam*** It's Miss Dawkins. She's having some trouble with a lock on a door in the basement. Can you have a look at it for her?

***Ben** turns to **Rosie**, who is also concerned.*

LIAM Jammed I'll bet. A drop of oil and a few magic words will open it. Be back soon.

He gets up.

PEGGY You could finish the tea.

LIAM Won't take a minute.

He goes out.

BEN *looking anxious* I've got to go.

ROSIE *firmly* You stay here.

BEN I'm going.

ROSIE Ben, stay here and finish your tea.

BEN *between gritted teeth* Rosie!

ROSIE Do you hear, Ben?

PEGGY Something the matter, Ben?

ROSIE No.

BEN No.

***Ben** stays. They continue the tea in silence.*

Music.

SCENE NINETEEN

The Hall of Allsprings House. **Liam** *and* **Gloria** *are heard offstage.*

LIAM   *singing* 'In Dublin's fair city, Where the girls are so pretty...'

GLORIA   Sssssh!

LIAM   Who's to hear? *Quieter* '...I first set my eyes on sweet Molly Malone. She wheeled her wheelbarrow...' *He stops* D'you know, this is a fine drop and it deserves a fine glass. Swiggin' from the bottle is not proper. The gentleman would not approve.

GLORIA   Sssssh! She sniggers

Liam enters followed by Gloria. Both are tipsy. Liam is holding an almost empty bottle of wine. Terry appears on the level above and watches them.

LIAM   *reading the label* Chateau Lafite something or other, 1926. *Kissing the bottle* There's a turn up for the books. Beautiful.

GLORIA   How many do you reckon there are down there?

LIAM   Who knows? We'll have to have another recce.

GLORIA   One shelf had 1870 on it. Not a big drinker, is he?

LIAM   We're helping him out in a small way. *He offers to fill her glass* Gloria, my dear.

He clicks his heels.

GLORIA   *giggling* Done like an officer. Would be better with a glass though.

LIAM   You're right. Dead right. Which way is it?

GLORIA   *pointing* Through there.

Liam goes through a door.

GLORIA   Not that one.

Lost momentarily in a world of her own, she begins to hum and make swaying movements as if dancing with someone.

Liam appears at the door wearing a World War One German uniform and helmet with spike. He parodies the German goose-step walk and salute.

LIAM   Would you believe it? There's a room full of

uniforms in there. *Mimicking a German accent he sings 'Lilli Marlene'* 'Underneath the Lamplight, By the barrack gate, Darling I remember...' *He moves towards her with stiff military bearing, still holding the bottle*

GLORIA   Oo-er! *She laughs and plays a simpering role* What big, shiny buttons, you've got.

LIAM   All ze better to dazzle your pretty little eyes, my dear. *By now they are close together* Would the lady care to dance?

GLORIA   Ooh! I don't know.

LIAM   Tonight we live, for tomorrow we must die.

GLORIA   Well then.

LIAM   *in his normal voice* Where's the wireless?

Gloria points to another room. Liam follows the direction off stage.

LIAM   *from the other room* Ah! Here's the thing hiding away.

Dance band music is heard from the wireless. Liam returns.

LIAM   Would the lady care to join me in a dance?

Liam whisks Gloria on to the 'dance floor' and they twirl around to the music. The war is forgotten. The music increases in volume and fills the space to create the feel of a ballroom.

Ben appears on the same level as Terry, but Terry's gaze is fixed on what is happening below. Liam and Gloria collapse in a heap. The radio goes fuzzy.

GLORIA   The orchestra's gone off key.

She goes out to fix it. Liam lies on his back, dizzy and drunk. Terry sees Ben and grabs him.

TERRY   Come here, you. I was right about your sister.

BEN   What?

TERRY   She's a traitor. A bloody little traitor.

BEN   I thought you'd be bothered about the room.

TERRY   That's safe. They found the other one with the wine in it. She's blabbed to her friend.

BEN   How do you know?

TERRY   I saw her.

BEN   She hasn't.

TERRY   If your sister has said anything, we're finished.

The enemy will get us. And if they do, I'll get you first, do you hear?

BEN   You've gone loopy.

*Terry pushes a fist threateningly up against **Ben's** face. The hall is silent. **Gloria** returns looking shocked and pale.*

GLORIA   Oh my God, they've bombed Coventry. Hundreds killed. It's terrible. The whole city's on fire. What are we doing? Drinking ourselves silly while people are dying.

Liam is brought to his senses. He staggers to his feet looking nervous.

LIAM   It'll be us next. Manchester, Liverpool. They'll incinerate us all. *In an effort to overcome his fear, he stands erect, looks around as if towards an audience and speaks in a grand, theatrical voice* Thank you, and goodnight.

Liam bows. They both go out

TERRY   *to **Ben*** You check with her to see if she's said anything. If she has...

Slides and sounds of the Coventry blitz.

SCENE TWENTY

*In the country. It is a sunny day with the sounds of a stream flowing and birdsong. **Margaret** is standing on the edge of the stream. Her spirits seem brighter, but **Rosie** is more preoccupied.*

MARGARET   You can see the fish. Hundreds of them. *She peers into the water* Look, a dragonfly!

ROSIE   Mm.

MARGARET   There are no streams like this anywhere near where I live. What about you?

ROSIE   The canal. But it's filthy dirty. You could die if you drink the water.

MARGARET   See how deep it is over there? In the middle. If we wait, we'll see a big fish swim through.

ROSIE   Mm.

MARGARET   You all right, Rosie?

ROSIE   Shall we have our sandwiches?
MARGARET   Yes, I'm hungry.

They sit on the bank and start to eat their sandwiches.

MARGARET   Listen. The birds.

They listen.

ROSIE   They never stop.

Pause.

MARGARET   It makes me sad.

Rosie looks at Margaret. Suddenly Margaret begins to sob.

ROSIE   What is it?
MARGARET   At home...
ROSIE   The bombs?

Margaret nods

ROSIE   Were they close?
MARGARET   They bombed our school. *Pause* Just one plane. On its own. A dive bomber, my dad said.
ROSIE   When?
MARGARET   During the daytime. The siren didn't go off.

Pause.

ROSIE   During lessons?
MARGARET   At lunchtime. My best friend was killed. And others too.
ROSIE   What was her name?
MARGARET   Frances. *Pause* I was lucky. That day I had a cold and my mum wouldn't let me go to school. I was cross because my class were going to see a play in the afternoon.
ROSIE   Frances, too?
MARGARET   Yes. She loved plays. We both did. Always acting and dressing up. We have a special box in her house for all our acting clothes.

Pause.

ROSIE   Would you rather go home now?
MARGARET   Not yet. *Pause* On the morning of the bomb, Frances called for me on the way to school. She had on a pair of gold shoes from the box. Her mum let her wear them as going to the play was special. I begged my mum to

let me go, but she said I'd pass my cold on to people, sitting next to them during the play. *Pause* We live opposite the school and I heard a siren miles away. In school they wouldn't have heard it. Playtime's always noisy. About a minute later there was this loud roaring sound but I didn't know it was a plane. Then the explosion. It shook the whole house. *Pause* My mum dashed out and I followed her. Fire engines came and there were people everywhere, but I managed to sneak through to the railings. *Pause* My teacher was trying to stop us looking. I could see them lying very still in the playground after the explosion. There were lots of people trying to help so I couldn't see everything. I moved along the railings a bit. And then I saw her, under a blanket. I knew it was Frances because I could see her shoes. *Pause* They'd been lined up ready to go to the play. And do you know what? It was a bright, sunny day like today. And quiet. After the bomb it was all quiet. Then after a while the birds started again. Singing. *Pause* I noticed that. I remember thinking they can keep on singing because they don't know what's happened. *Pause* Sometimes I lie awake at night thinking about it. My friends are dead but I'm alive. *Pause* I can't tell people.

ROSIE   About how you feel?

MARGARET   Not that. They don't know.

ROSIE   Know what?

MARGARET   I could have saved them. The siren, you see. I heard it, they didn't. If I'd run to the school and told them, they would have got to the shelters. There was time to do it. *Pause* I haven't ever told anybody about the siren.

ROSIE   Perhaps you... *She can't think what to say* It's getting dark.

MARGARET   Shall we go?

ROSIE   We can stay a little longer if you like.

MARGARET   We'll go. Rosie, it's easy talking to you. With adults you can't say what you feel – they say that you have to be strong.

ROSIE   Margaret, do you want to stay at my house tonight?

MARGARET   Oh yes.

ROSIE   You can have my bed. I'll sleep on some cushions.

MARGARET   Will that be all right?

ROSIE   I'll ask Peggy. She won't mind.

They leave.

SCENE TWENTY-ONE

Outside the basement room in Allsprings House. **Terry** *is holding* **Ben** *in a threatening way.*

BEN   She hasn't said anything. Honest.
TERRY   I don't believe you.
BEN   You've got to. It's the truth.

Ben *is near to tears.*

TERRY   There's worse now. They've been in the room.
BEN   *astonished, disbelieving* What? They can't have. How?
TERRY   There must be another key. Got in while I wasn't looking. Cunning, the two of 'em.
BEN   Rosie hasn't been in here, I know it. She would have told me.

Terry *unlocks the door to the room.*

TERRY   You'll see.

Ben *goes in, followed by* **Terry.**

BEN   What have they done?
TERRY   Things have been moved.
BEN   This is how it was when we left.
TERRY   It's changed. Only a bit, but I can tell.
BEN   You're mad, Terry. You're making it all up.
TERRY   She's blabbed, hasn't she? Well? *He gives* **Ben** *a stabbing punch* She's blabbed the lot to her friend, and now they've been in here.
BEN   They haven't. I know Rosie won't tell. She promised.
TERRY   I saw her with the letter, showing it to the other girl. The secret's out.
BEN   Terry...
TERRY   Unless it's you. You've been in here for them.
BEN   *finding courage in his desperation* Don't be stupid.
TERRY   Are you their spy, Ben? Switched sides, have you? *He gives* **Ben** *another stabbing punch*
BEN   You stop that.
TERRY   You're their spy.
BEN   I'm not.
TERRY   They're talking secrets, I know it.
BEN   What?

TERRY   And they've tricked you to go in with them.
BEN   You're cracked.
TERRY   You're on their side, not mine.
BEN   Maybe I am.
TERRY   Right, you're going to get it.
BEN   *brazenly* Get what?
TERRY   You know, and if you don't you soon will.

He gives another punch, harder this time.

BEN   Yes, and I've got a secret to tell you.
TERRY   *with a punch to punctuate each word* What's that?
BEN   I know something about your mum.
TERRY   Eh?
BEN   I know what's happened to her.

SCENE TWENTY-TWO

The kitchen in Peggy's House. **Liam** *enters, looking depressed. He stands still, lost in thought. Then he extends an arm and watches his hand, which begins to shake involuntarily. He turns to look at himself in the mirror, stands to attention, and sings in full voice.*

LIAM   'I wish I was in Carrickfergus, Only for a night in Ballygrand. I would swim over the deepest ocean, Only for a night in Ballygrand.'

Angie enters and is immediately busy.

ANGIE   What brought this on?
LIAM   Oh nothing, nothing. *Watching* **Angie** What brought you home?
ANGIE   We're going on full alert after the Coventry business. Round the clock from now on. I may have to stay over at the Barracks.

She moves in and out collecting clothes, etc.

ANGIE   There's another reason, too. Guess what? Forbes-Lomax has been decorated out in the desert. Took an enemy tank unit by surprise and won a complete surrender. I can just see him, charging across the deserts of Africa in his tank, roaring orders. The war will run out before he does.

Pause.

LIAM   Your ack-ack guns at the ready, too? Primed and polished?

Angie *stops to look at* **Liam.**

ANGIE   Your boots could do with some attention. They're looking a bit scuffed. Clumsy dancer, is she?
LIAM   Eh?
ANGIE   Miss Dawkins.

Liam *looks embarrassed.*

LIAM   Spies everywhere, these days.
ANGIE   Well?
LIAM   No, no. As a matter of fact, she is very nimble on her feet.
ANGIE   She may need to be. To escape from unwelcome approaches.
LIAM   Maybe. On the other hand not every approach is unwelcome.
ANGIE   Why were you singing when I came in?
LIAM   The medical check up.
ANGIE   You sing about seeing the doctor?
LIAM   Of course. Something to sing about. Fit, you see. Fighting fit, I am. Well, aren't you pleased? Back to the action and all that.
ANGIE   How long before you have to go?
LIAM   A few days.
ANGIE   Not long for you to get used to the idea.
LIAM   Except I knew. Didn't need a doctor to tell me. *Pause* Marching off to glory loses some of its appeal second time round. *He takes a letter from his pocket* From Mrs Parks. Just as I said. She wants the children back home. I'll take them back to Manchester with me when I go.

Pause

ANGIE   All change, eh? I won't be long here either. As soon as I've got some experience on the battery here, they'll post me somewhere else. The war's moving fast.

Peggy *is heard coming in.*

ANGIE   I'm going to be late.

She goes out to finish gathering what she needs. **Peggy** *enters and fixes a determined look on* **Liam.**

LIAM   Well?

PEGGY   I'm going to the factory.

LIAM   An awful time of day to start work.

PEGGY   The early night shift. But, it will be my last.

LIAM   Night shift?

PEGGY   Any shift. I've decided. So there.

LIAM   Taking control, eh? *Pause* Peggy, there's something you must know about Terry.

PEGGY   I know it. The whole story. I've just seen the Billeting Officer.

LIAM   Well?

PEGGY   Angie in?

LIAM   Yes.

PEGGY   Better tell her.

LIAM   Tell her what?

*Peggy goes out. **Liam** is alone in the silence, not quite sure what might happen next. He begins to sing the second part of his song.*

LIAM   'But the sea is wide and I cannot swim over, Nor have I wings so I could fly. I wish I could find me a handy boatman, Who'd carry me over to my love and I.'

*The voices of **Peggy** and **Angie** are heard offstage getting louder and louder.*

ANGIE   *offstage* Terry?

PEGGY   ...just to find out if there are any spare billets.

ANGIE   And there are some?

PEGGY   Yes, but I haven't decided. It's difficult.

ANGIE   That and your job. You giving up altogether?

PEGGY   Angie, let me explain.

ANGIE   I can't believe it. What's got into you?

*Angie storms into the room. **Liam** stops singing.*

ANGIE   *to **Liam*** How can she do it? Her husband is out there putting his life on the line and she's giving up the lot.

Peggy enters behind.

ANGIE   Peggy, it hasn't sunk in with you yet, has it? The war. I know it's grim, and it's awful, but it's happening. Not just over there, in other countries, but here, at home, and it's getting closer day by day. Bristol, Birmingham, Coventry. Where next, Peggy? People are giving their lives to stop Hitler. Ordinary people, not looking for glory.

Peggy, have you thought for a moment of what might happen to us if we lose this war? Do you want to be ruled by Hitler? What's happening in the war is more important than wall flowers in the back garden and mother's meetings at the church hall. Look, I don't mind these things. You want them? Fine. But if you want to keep them, you've got to fight for them, like everybody else, and your job and all the other work you do is going to help. *Pause – **Angie's** tone changes* Peggy, I know how it is, not hearing anything. If letters came and you knew he was all right, everything would seem different, I know that. It's hard, but there are other people with worse things to think about. *Pause* Oh, Peggy.

Angie puts her arms around her.

PEGGY   If you'd give me a minute to explain.
ANGIE   I have to go. It's a full alert. I don't know when I'll be off duty. Bye.

She goes out.

LIAM   My fault. I take the blame. I put you up to it.
PEGGY   She makes me feel like a traitor. This time she's wrong.
LIAM   Should have let you have your say, mind. Went too far, she did. You have your reasons. She's on edge. You may want the action, but when it comes, that feeling in the stomach...
PEGGY   Time to go. Rosie and Ben should be told they're going back to Manchester.
LIAM   Yes.
PEGGY   The sooner the better.
LIAM   I'll go and tell them now.

They both go out together.

SCENE TWENTY-THREE

*Outside Peggy's house. **Rosie** and **Margaret** enter.*

MARGARET   I'll wait outside while you ask.
ROSIE   It's all right.
MARGARET   No, I'd rather.
ROSIE   I won't be a minute.

Rosie goes inside. She looks around the house calling as she goes.

ROSIE   Peggy...Peggy...Liam...Angie.

*She goes out of sight to the back of the house. **Margaret** stays outside.*

***Ben** emerges from Allsprings House. His face is bruised and his lip cut.*

BEN   *to **Margaret*** Where's Rosie?
MARGARET   In the house. What's the matter?
BEN   Can you get Rosie?

***Margaret** sees that **Ben** is in trouble and rushes to the front door.*

MARGARET   Rosie?

***Rosie** appears immediately.*

ROSIE   They're not here. Peggy must be at work. Uncle Liam's not here, either.
MARGARET   Rosie, your brother needs help.

Rosie** runs across to **Ben.

ROSIE   What happened Ben? Terry? Terry did it, didn't he?

***Ben** nods.*

ROSIE   You haven't seen Uncle Liam? Angie?
BEN   No.

***Terry** appears at the entrance to Allsprings House.*

ROSIE   *to **Terry*** You've half killed him, you great bully. What happened? I'm going to the police about you.
TERRY   *obsessively* A traitor, you are. It's your fault. You made a promise. You've got a key. Been inside. Told everything. Now they'll get us. The enemy knows all about us.
ROSIE   What are you going on about?
TERRY   Come inside and I'll show you.
ROSIE   No.
TERRY   *pointing to **Margaret*** She's stays out.
ROSIE   Don't be stupid. I'm not coming in.
BEN   Please Rosie. Do as he says. It'll be the worse for us if you don't.

ROSIE   *to **Terry*** I'm not scared of you.

***Terry** grabs **Ben** who yells with fear.*

TERRY   Inside.
ROSIE   You dare touch him again.
BEN   Please, Rosie. Please.
TERRY   I won't touch him if you come.
ROSIE   After, I'm getting the police.
TERRY   The other girl stays out. Tell her to turn round.

***Margaret** turns round so as not to make things worse.*

ROSIE   Don't worry, Margaret. I'll be out in a minute.

***Terry** retreats into Allsprings House still holding on to **Ben**.
Rosie follows. **Margaret** waits till she is sure they have gone,
then ventures over but dares not go inside Allsprings. She goes
to Peggy's front door.*

MARGARET   PEGGY! LIAM! ANGIE!

*No reply. The house is silent. She comes out, but can't think of
what to do. She sits down, looking very anxious.*

*The drone of planes returns and continues through the next
scene.*

SCENE TWENTY-FOUR

*The basement room in Allsprings House. **Rosie** is looking
around the room. **Terry** has released **Ben** and is standing
close to the door which is shut.*

TERRY   Well?
ROSIE   Well what?
TERRY   Things have been moved. You told her the secret,
and you've been in here.
ROSIE   You'll be in real trouble.
TERRY   We promised to protect everything. They're his
things, not ours. We said nothing's to be touched till he
comes home.
ROSIE   Listen, you bully, I haven't been near this room
since you made me do that silly swearing.
TERRY   You found another key. I can tell when
somebody's been snooping.

ROSIE   *now furious* There is no other key. No spies. Nobody cares a damn about what's in here except you. Look, I'll show you what I think about these precious things.

She picks up a cabinet and is about to throw it, but **Terry** *snatches* **Ben** *and holds him threateningly.*

TERRY   You do that and he gets it again.

Rosie stops.

ROSIE   Right, you great bully, beating up people who are younger then you. What happened, Ben?
TERRY   He was telling lies. Both of you, liars.
ROSIE   What about?
TERRY   Telling lies about my mother.

Pause.

ROSIE   Ben?
BEN   The Billeting Officer. She came to the house to tell Peggy. I heard what she said.

Pause. **Rosie** *looks at* **Terry** *who is still clinging on to* **Ben.**

ROSIE   *to* **Ben** Ben, did you make any of it up?

Ben *daren't answer.*

ROSIE   BEN, tell me.
BEN   No.

Rosie *looks at* **Terry.** *For the first time he looks vulnerable.*

Sounds of laughter from **Liam** *and* **Gloria** *in the wine cellar next door, muffled by the thick wall in between.* **Liam** *begins to sing.*

LIAM   'I'll take you home again Kathleen, To where your heart will feel no pain. And when the fields are fresh and green, I will take you to your home Kathleen.'
ROSIE   *over the song* It's Uncle Liam and Gloria. *Shouting on impulse* LIAM! Help!
TERRY   Shut up! Shut up!

At the climax of the song there is a huge crash. **Liam** *has fallen into the wine racks, knocking them over. Then all is silent.*

ROSIE   *shouting again* LIAM! LIAM!

There is no response.

TERRY   He can't get in anyway. The door's locked.

*He shows **Rosie** the key. **Rosie,** in a sudden fit of anger, throws herself at **Terry** who has to release **Ben** to defend himself. She lashes at him with punches and **Terry** hits back. **Ben** becomes distraught.*

BEN   Rosie! Stop it! Stop it!

The air raid siren goes off. The fight halts.

ROSIE   Now, we've got to get out.
TERRY   We're staying here.
ROSIE   The shelter. We've got to get to the shelter. *Calling* LIAM!

Still no response.

TERRY   It's safer here. Strong walls and roof.
BEN   *beginning to panic* Let us out Terry, please!
TERRY   No.
ROSIE   I can hear something.

*She pushes her way past **Terry** to the door and puts her ear to it.*

ROSIE   It's Gloria calling for Margaret. *Shouting* Help! Help!

She listens. No reply.

TERRY   Drunk.
ROSIE   Give me the key, Terry. Give me the key.

__Terry__ hangs on grimly to the key.

TERRY   No key. No point shouting. We stay here till it's over.
BEN   Try shouting again, Rosie.

__Rosie__ listens again at the door.

ROSIE   I can still hear her. *Calling* Gloria! *She listens* She's going further away.

The siren stops.

__Terry__ switches out the light.

BEN   What did you do that for?

TERRY   Don't want any stray light.
ROSIE   There can't be any.
TERRY   Through the grill. A tight blackout.
BEN   Are the planes going to Manchester, Rosie?

No reply. The drone of planes grows louder, becoming more like actual massed planes. This continues throughout the next scene, the sound increasing in volume as the planes approach.

SCENE TWENTY-FIVE

*Peggy's House. **Margaret** is alone still, but now frantic with worry. She has gone into the house in the vain hope that someone has returned.*

MARGARET   *Calling* LIAM! PEGGY!

She rushes around the house in panic.

*The **A.R.P. Warden** enters and checks the house.*

A.R.P. WARDEN   Hey! Kill that light! There's a raid on!

***Margaret** rushes out to him.*

MARGARET   Where are Peggy and Liam?
A.R.P. WARDEN   Who? I don't know. Never mind them, you should be in that shelter.
MARGARET   My friends are in the house over there. I don't know where they are.

*She grabs the **Warden's** sleeve and drags him towards Allsprings.*

A.R.P. WARDEN   Hey you. Cut that out. Get into the shelter. Go on.

She keeps dragging him.

MARGARET   There's no shelter in the house. They must get out.

*The planes are almost overhead. The ack-ack guns start firing. They are very loud. **Margaret** and the **Warden** can be heard only between the bursts of fire.*

A.R.P. WARDEN   I've no time to go searching the house. My first duty is to the people in the street.

MARGARET   Please, please. I don't know where they are.

The sound of a dive bomber. **Margaret** *looks up.*

A.R.P. WARDEN   Get into the bloody shelter!

Long fire from the guns. The dive bomber swoops over, machine gunning all the way.

Margaret *keeps pulling at the* **Warden.**

A.R.P. WARDEN   Get off me. Let me go. *He tries to shake himself free* Look, if you haven't got the sense to get into the shelter...

He frees himself and runs off. **Margaret** *stands transfixed with terror.*

The planes are directly overhead. The dive bomber can be heard high above preparing for another dive. Lights focus to a single spot on **Margaret.** *She looks up the beam as if towards the plane. The plane goes into a dive getting louder as it approaches target. The ack-ack guns fire continuously.*

MARGARET   *shouting hysterically* ROSIE! BEN!

She rushes off to Allsprings. Lights fade but the sounds of the bomber and the guns increase. There is a great explosion in the darkness.

Before the sounds of the explosion die away, music fades in. It is a big dance band playing a popular tune as if in a darkened dance hall. The sound swells and continues for some time, creating a bridge to the next scene.

SCENE TWENTY-SIX

Peggy's house. The music fades to a small sound coming from a radio at the back of the room. **Rosie** *and* **Ben** *are sitting on their suitcases ready for departure to the station. They stare into the distance as if still in shock.* **Terry** *is sitting at the table.* **Liam,** *grim faced, is tying his kit bag. A long tableau.* **Peggy** *comes in. She is the only sign of activity in the house.*

PEGGY   *to* **Liam** I wanted the news. *She turns the radio off* It's no more than 20 minutes to the station. You're in good time. Angie's coming to give you a hand with the cases. *Pause* A mercy that Rosie and Ben's parents are safe.

Liam hears, but offers no response. He sits on his kit bag and puts his face in his hands.

PEGGY *Sympathetically* Don't be too hard on yourself. It was chance, an accident. *Pause* You might all have been killed. The rescue services had almost given up hope of finding survivors.

Pause.

LIAM I could have avoided it.

No reply from Peggy.

LIAM You think so, too, I know.

Peggy looks at the bruises on Ben's face.

PEGGY They'll take some time to heal. What your mother is going to say, I daren't imagine. *Showing Ben's face to Liam* Terry did this. All to do with the room in the basement.

TERRY *to Ben* You needn't have told.

BEN I'll get back at you, Terry. I'll find a way.

PEGGY *to Terry* The least you can do is to apologise to him.

Terry turns away. Peggy looks at Liam.

PEGGY I've just telephoned Mrs Parks. She won't let them stay here.

LIAM And she won't let them stay there.

PEGGY I suggested North Wales. She's making some enquiries.

Rosie looks at her, having heard this.

PEGGY *to Rosie* She'll work something out.

Silence. The same tableau of figures.

A knock on the door.

PEGGY *calling* Come in. It's open.

The A.R.P.Warden enters.

A.R.P. WARDEN They've taken the girl to the hospital in Chester. She'll be all right. Broken legs, bad concussion. A month in hospital, they reckon.

***Rosie** suddenly bursts out in sobs of relief. **Peggy** comforts her.*

PEGGY   You thought it might have been worse, didn't you?

***Rosie** nods.*

PEGGY   *to the **Warden*** What about her Aunt Gloria?

A.R.P. WARDEN   The body's at the undertaker's. Funeral in London, I suppose, as soon as they can get her back. What a business, eh?

ROSIE   Will we be able to visit Margaret in hospital?

PEGGY   I hope so.

A.R.P. WARDEN   Silly girl, she is. Her own fault. I told her to get in the shelter, but she'd have none of it.

PEGGY   We have to get these people to the...

A.R.P. WARDEN   *turning his attention to the children* You young ones showed great presence of mind, staying put in the basement room like that. Amazing, isn't it? All them paintings, vases, statues, not a scratch on any of them. The house is demolished, well, as good as, and everything saved. A good shelter, all right. *Turning to **Liam** with a sarcastic look* Kids are smarter than adults sometimes.

***Liam** re-ties his kit bag.*

*Another knock on the door. The **Billeting Officer** enters.*

BILLETING OFFICER   I hope you don't mind me taking the liberty, but the door was open...

PEGGY   No, no. *to the **Warden*** Thank you for coming.

BILLETING OFFICER   It's a difficult time for you, I know, but I thought best to bring it to you straight away.

PEGGY   What's that?

BILLETING OFFICER   A letter for Terry. They found his dad.

***Terry** looks across at them. **The Billeting Officer** gives the letter to **Peggy**.*

BILLETING OFFICER   Now, about the other business. There are three possible billets.

PEGGY   Please, they are all about to leave for the station. Could you call back in a few minutes. Thanks.

BILLETING OFFICER   Of course. I didn't mean to...

PEGGY   Thank you, we won't be long.

Peggy and the **Billeting Officer** go out.

Pause.

A.R.P. WARDEN   *to* **Liam** Sleep well? The way to do it, eh? Knock yourself out with a bottle of good wine and wake up when the trouble's gone.

Liam ties his bag for the third time. **Peggy** comes back in.

PEGGY   Angie's here.
A.R.P. WARDEN   She must be feeling a bit pleased. Scoring a hit with her first effort.
PEGGY   If she is, she isn't showing it.
A.R.P. WARDEN   They reckon the guns caught the wing tip so it couldn't pull out of the dive in time.
PEGGY   *showing the* **Warden** *to the door* Thank you for bringing us the news.

Angie enters.

A.R.P. WARDEN   Here she is. Your hit confirmed yet?
ANGIE   *subdued* No. *To the others* All set? It's not a long walk.
A.R.P. WARDEN   *to* **Angie** Manchester got a real pounding. This is just the beginning, you mark my words.

He leaves.

LIAM   *to* **Rosie** *and* **Ben** Ready?
ANGIE   *to* **Liam** They'll feel better when they get home. See their mother and father.

Liam picks up the cases. Pause.

ANGIE   *to* **Peggy** The Billeting Officer was leaving as I arrived. You're going through with it?
PEGGY   Angie, listen...I'm not going to the factory any more. Please, you must believe me. *Pause* I know you think I'm wrong. I've been to see about another job in town. Please, Angie...you're my sister.

Angie looks directly at **Peggy**. She then turns to **Terry** as if to say 'what about him?'

PEGGY   I don't know yet.

Pause.

ANGIE   We'd better get going.
LIAM   *to* **Rosie** *and* **Ben** Time to say cheerio to Terry.

ROSIE   *doing her duty* Bye, Terry.
TERRY   *with only a brief glance towards her* Bye.
LIAM   Ben?

Ben *says nothing.*

LIAM   Bye, Terry.
PEGGY   I'll come with you to the door.

Angie *turns to* ***Peggy*** *and gives her a big, warm hug.*

ANGIE   I'm sorry. Too inclined to see things my way.

Peggy *looks more relieved. They all go out. At the door,* ***Peggy*** *turns to* ***Terry.***

PEGGY   I forgot. Here.

She gives him the letter from his father and goes out. ***Terry,*** *now alone, looks at the letter as if worried about its contents. After a few moments he puts it down on the table.* ***Peggy*** *returns.*

PEGGY   They've gone.

She sits down at the table opposite ***Terry*** *and for a while is lost in thought. She 'comes to', and sees the unopened letter on the table.*

PEGGY   You haven't opened it.

Terry *shakes his head. Pause.*

PEGGY   Do you want me to?
TERRY   No.
PEGGY   Terry, it's from your father.
TERRY   I know.
PEGGY   I think we should. *Pause* Well?
TERRY   If you like.

Peggy *hands him the letter.*

PEGGY   Here.
TERRY   No, you.

Peggy *opens the letter.* ***Terry*** *looks around, as if not interested.*

PEGGY   Shall I read it?

Terry *gives a shrug.*

PEGGY   Dear Terry, I am sorry I have not been in touch with you for a while, but I am glad to hear you are well. I am also glad they have fetched you out of Manchester because of the bombs. I hope the people you live with are kind to you and you are all right. As for me, I have got a new job. It is in the kitchens at the army camp in Catterick. It is not a bad job, but I can't do much else with my eyes being like they are. Perhaps someday I will be able to come to see you where you are now. I am sending you some money to buy yourself something. Look after yourself and keep well. Yours, Dad.

Pause.

PEGGY   Did you know where your dad was before this letter?

Terry shrugs.

PEGGY   Better to face the truth in the end. Not a sniper...but still doing his bit. *Pause* Look on the good side. He may come and see you.
TERRY   Maybe.
PEGGY   The room was for him? A place to stay?
TERRY   Ben. He's a blabber.
PEGGY   You hurt him badly.

Pause. A knock on the door.

PEGGY   The Billeting Officer.

Peggy and Terry face each other across the table. Another knock.

PEGGY   Angie will be posted soon. She hasn't said, but I know. *Pause* I hate this war. But it's here. *Pause* Well, Terry. There's an empty room upstairs. *Pause* You've got it to yourself...if you like.

Another knock.

PEGGY   Well? Shall I tell her to go, or come in? Terry?

Terry shrugs, giving nothing away. Pause.

PEGGY   To go?

Terry nods. Peggy gets up and goes out. Terry, alone, looks round the room.

Lights fade to spot on Terry. Sound of birdsong. Spot gradually fades.

Birdsong continues, then fades.

STAGING THE PLAY

As most of the action takes place in two separate locations –
Peggy's house and Allsprings house – you could set them at
either end of the acting area, facing each other. The open
acting area in between the locations could then form part of
both sets as needed. So when Rosie, Ben and Terry are
'digging for victory', the area becomes the front garden of
Peggy's house. When they are exploring Allsprings, it changes
to the main hall with the paintings of the Forbes-Lomax
family.

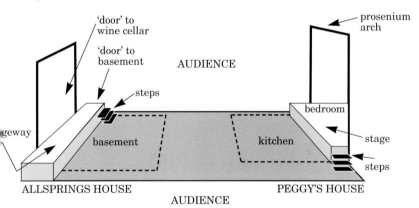

If you are performing the play in a school hall with a
proscenium arch, you could set all the main action on the floor
level along the length of the hall, with Peggy's house at the
stage end. The level of the stage could then be used for the
bedroom in Peggy's house and the steps to the stage could be
the stairs in her house. At the opposite end of the acting area,
Allsprings house could be set out with the basement on floor
level and a set of steps leading up to the imaginary door of the
basement and rostra which form the passageway.

The dotted lines on the diagram above represent the
'invisible walls' of Peggy's house and Allsprings basement. A
simple way of showing these walls is to stick lines of white

71

PVC electrical tape onto the floor. You can make a straight line with the tape by sticking the first inch of the tape to the floor at one end of the 'wall', unravelling the tape to the length required, stretching it slightly, and then lowering it so that all the tape touches the floor at the same time. Doors can be represented by leaving gaps in the tape and adding small right angle turns.

The two ends of the set should be visually very different. Peggy's house is bright, clean and open, and very neat. The basement in Allsprings is much darker, and has a chilly, dank feel. Bits of junk and old furniture are piled up which in the darkness make mysterious and eerie shapes. During the play, Terry and Ben gradually transform the look of the basement as they bring in clean furniture, paintings, and ornaments from the rest of the house, and sort out the junk to make the room more habitable.

PROJECTING PICTURES

Many stages in schools have a back wall painted white for slide projection. If you place the upper floor of Peggy's house on the stage level, the back wall will provide an ideal screen for the projected pictures. By plugging the projector into a lighting circuit, you will be able to gain effect by fading the pictures in and out on the dimmer board.

LIGHTING

The brightest parts of the set will be Peggy's house and the central area. If you can, use a variety of colour gels in the spotlights to create the effect of sunshine. You could use just a single dim bulb for the Allsprings basement to create a dingy atmosphere, and the passageway could have only enough light to pick out the shapes of moving figures.

In some scenes you could use particular lights for dramatic effect – for example, in the basement during the air-raid, a single torch lighting the children will help to convey their fear and isolation.

If you have enough dimmers for your lights, control each acting area separately. A good general rule is to avoid blackouts if you can as this could make the audience feel the drama has stopped.

SOUND EFFECTS

Sound effects are a vital element in the play. Nothing is more evocative of the Second World War than the sounds of air-raid sirens, the drone of bombers, and popular songs and radio programmes from the time.

Some of the most popular songs of the time were *The White Cliffs of Dover*, *A Nightingale Sang in Berkeley Square* and *We'll Meet Again*, usually sung by Vera Lynn, 'the Forces' Sweetheart'. In *The Birds Keep On Singing* there are some places in the text where music is suggested. You may wish to include music elsewhere to link scenes or to add dramatic effect.

All the voice extracts in the playscript are taken from a cassette tape of a compilation of original recordings called *The Second World War*, from the BBC Radio Collection. This tape can be bought in record shops, or you should be able to borrow it from your local library. As the recorded material is copyright, you must first get permission if you want to use it in a production which is to be performed to a public audience. This is a normal procedure with copyright material, and all you need to do is to write to BBC Enterprises Ltd, 80 Wood Lane, London, W12 0TT (or telephone 0181 743 5588) explaining how and why you want to use extracts from the tapes. You will *not* need to gain permission to use the recordings for class work or for any performance which is not open to the public.

If you can, place the sound system speakers in the stage set so that the radio voices can sometimes be heard as if they are coming from the radio on the set, but at other times spread to fill the whole auditorium.

Original recordings of World War II sounds – sirens, ack-ack guns, massed planes and dive bombers – are available in the BBC Sound Effects Series, record number 126M. As copyright rules do not apply to these sound effects, you may use them for public performance without gaining permission from the BBC. Remember to set your playback levels carefully for the performance. So, for example, the birdsong in the final moment of the play should be very quiet, perhaps just audible, as if it were a distant 'echo' of the scene in the country. In contrast, the guns in the scene before should have a big booming effect, but not to the point where it is painful for the audience.

PROPS AND COSTUMES

One of the most creative aspects of producing the play will be building an authentic wartime look. You may have to search a little for props and furniture that are from the period. Rather than trying to create everything in realistic detail, concentrate on a few key objects – radio, sideboard, gas masks.

Costumes should be a little easier to find. Many people store away old clothes and are often happy to see them used in a play. Try and find clothes from jumble sales and car boot sales that could be adapted. You will be able to find pictorial information about wartime fashion in your local library. Uniforms can be obtained from ex-army stores, or directly from the army.

The turban

Women's hairstyles are very important in creating a wartime look. Many women tied their hair up in a 'turban' using a headscarf. It was a very practical style at a time when getting on with war work was more important than how you looked.

THE START OF THE PERFORMANCE

Before the play begins, create an atmosphere that evokes the wartime period, and helps the audience to 'travel back' in time. There are a number of ways you can do this:

- show slides of a variety of aspects of life during the war;
- play a sequence of music and radio from the period;
- set a few spotlights to pick out some parts of the set;
- dress programme sellers and helpers in wartime costumes;
- display posters and pictures from wartime.

IDEAS AND RESOURCES FOR WORK ON THE PLAY

THE EVACUATION

On Friday, 1st September, 1939, children in cities throughout the country were woken early, dressed and taken to school where they assembled in the playground. Each of them carried a gas mask and a suitcase or bag containing clothes. The teachers gave them an armband and a label for identification, and emergency rations which included a tin of corned beef, some sweets and a bar of chocolate. Then they marched off towards the nearest station to tearful farewells from their parents. It was a hot and sunny day. Some of the children carried buckets and spades thinking they were going on holiday to the seaside.

Evacuees at Paddington Station

At the station the children poured into waiting trains. None of them, including the teachers, had any idea of where they were going. Destinations had been kept secret. Very few of the children had ever been away from home before, or even been on a train, but now they were embarking on a journey of perhaps a hundred miles or more to live with strangers.

On the same day, Hitler's forces invaded Poland. Two days later, at 11 o'clock in the morning, the British ultimatum (final demand, with a time limit) to Hitler to withdraw his troops from Poland ran out, and the British Prime Minister, Neville Chamberlain, announced to the Nation, from 10 Downing Street, that Britain was at war with Germany. The evacuation came as no surprise to the children, or their parents. They had been rehearsing the plan for weeks. During the two years before war broke out, the Government was very concerned about the dangers of gas attacks and air raids. They knew that in this war, unlike previous wars, citizens at home would be a target of enemy attack. The Government decided that it would therefore be necessary to move children away from the cities to safer areas in the country.

The government evacuation scheme separated children from their families for several months or even years. Some mothers who did not want to be separated from their children were evacuated with them.

WARTIME EVENTS IN THE PLAY

When you do some background reading about the Second World War, you will notice that wartime events which in reality were a long time apart are fitted into a short time period in the play. Terry and the Parks family leave Manchester at the beginning of the war in September 1939, and their experiences away from home occur over a few weeks only. They are affected, however, by events which actually happened much later in the war. So, for example, the evacuation of Dunkirk – the reason for Liam's return home from the war – actually took place nine months later, in June 1940. Large scale bombing of English cities began with the mass raid on London docks on 7 September, 1940. The big raid on Coventry occurred two months later on 14 November, and Manchester was hit in December of the same year.

The difference between the two time scales will not be a problem in a performance of the play. Theatre is not restricted by natural time in this way. The audience is more interested in the story than keeping a check on whether the events fit accurately with historical time.

TERRY AND THE PARKS FAMILY

In the evacuation, most children were parted from their mothers who had to stay behind. Many mothers found the separation too painful and took the first opportunity to bring their children home. Just a few parents saw the evacuation as a way of getting rid of unwanted offspring. Terry is one of those unfortunates. As soon as he is sent away from Manchester, his mother leaves home to start a new life for herself. At the other extreme is Mrs Parks, whose concern for Rosie and Ben is such that she decides to be evacuated with them. This must have been a difficult decision for her to make. It also causes a problem for the Billeting Officer as places in homes for evacuees were in short supply. It was not usual for mothers to accompany older children.

Written work

Imagine that before the evacuation Terry has been absent frequently from school and is showing no interest in school work. In pairs, imagine you are his social workers, and write a report on Terry which may help to explain his behaviour. The report could be given verbally to a small group of Terry's teachers.

Drama

1 In the play, it is discovered that Terry's mother has moved. In pairs, role play a meeting between the local official making enquiries, and a neighbour who knows something (though probably not everything) about the situation.
2 In the same pairs, role play a scene between Mr and Mrs Parks before the final call for the evacuation, where they discuss what they think will be the best arrangement for their family. As the play tells you little about Mr Parks, try to discover more in this improvisation.
3 Imagine that before the evacuation begins, Mrs Parks first tried to billet Rosie and Ben with her sister who lives in the country. The sister has spare rooms, but thinks that the two

children could be a heavy responsibility, especially as the war may go on for a long time. Improvise the scene in which Mrs Parks and her sister meet to discuss the problem.

THE BILLETING OFFICER

Well before the evacuation took place, Billeting Officers had to do an accommodation survey of houses in their areas. Families that had spaces were obliged to take in evacuees, even if they didn't want to. The Government gave 8 shillings and sixpence a week (42p) towards feeding and clothing each evacuee.

Billeting officer

Drama

1 In pairs. The Officer calls on Peggy before the evacuation to ask about accommodation she has available. Peggy is very unhappy about the prospect of having evacuees, but the Billeting Officer is a government official and has authority to make her take them. As this scene happens before the war, it could include a third character, Peggy's husband Danny. Though he would expect to be away in the war, he would probably have an opinion on what might be best for Peggy and the war effort.

2 In groups of four, role play a scene involving the Billeting Officer with Mrs Parks, Rosie and Ben, who have just arrived. The Billeting officer was not expecting to have to find places for mothers of older children, and more children have arrived than expected. How is she going to cope?

PEGGY AND WAR WORK

Among women between eighteen and forty, about nine out of ten who were single, and eight out of ten who were married took jobs in the forces or in industry. Many welcomed the opportunity to work and to earn better money than they could in peacetime, but others did it because they were directed to do so by the government. Women could avoid war work only if they had heavy family responsibilities. Those that did not join the forces took jobs in industry, transport or agriculture. They trained as welders, lathe and drill operators, mechanics, machinists and drivers, or worked on farms as general labourers in the 'Land Army'.

Woman doing war work

Peggy could not have claimed exemption from war work as she had no family of her own, but being married, she would not have been expected to be 'mobile' like many young unmarried women, and to take up employment in other areas of the country where workers were needed.

Women became highly skilled at tasks which before the war had been regarded as men's work. In the factories, however, the shifts were 12 hours long, and the work repetitive. Through exhaustion and boredom, many women came to feel that what they were doing was of no immediate use to the war effort. Many women in industry during the war were interviewed as part of a government scheme called Mass-Observation. One woman, Sadie, aged 20, had to leave home at half past six in the morning and walk into town to get a bus to the factory. She did not get back till half past nine at night:

'It's wicked the hours we work here. I don't know any other factory that works like we do. I can't hardly get myself out of bed in the mornings. I could lay my head down on this bench this minute, and not wake up till eight o'clock. I could, honest.'

In some factories, the attitudes of the men towards the women made matters worse. The charge hands (supervisors), almost all of them men, tended to treat the women as scatter-brained nitwits who couldn't do anything right. Sometimes, for a joke, the women would pretend to get things wrong to see how the charge hand would react.

Drama

1 Read Peggy's story in scene 3 about her machine getting stuck. Then recreate the incident in the factory, but as if a group of women workers are playing a trick on Popeye, the charge hand.

2 How would the charge hand treat Peggy if she asked for a little extra time off because she has got too tired? In pairs, improvise the scene. This could perhaps take place after Popeye has found out that the women have been playing tricks on him.

3 In small groups, create a series of six tableaux (a freeze frame of a scene) depicting the life of domestic bliss that Peggy thinks she may have had if the war had not disrupted her life. The series could start with a wedding picture, and include different aspects of the life of a housewife. Women's magazines from the period will give you a clear idea of what the woman's life in the home was like and what her main concerns were about her family. Turn two of your tableaux into 'clips' from scenes by introducing words and actions.

Written work

Imagine that at the end of the play, when Peggy has decided that Terry should stay, she writes a letter to Danny. Write this letter thinking about how much she would reveal of what has happened and of her concerns about the future. Perhaps by now she understands that their lives have been changed and can never return to the way they were before the war.

ANGIE AND WAR WORK IN THE FORCES

Angie is a member of Auxiliary Territorial Service (ATS). The two other military services for women were the Women's Royal Naval Service (WRNS), and the Women's Auxiliary Air Force (WAAF). During the war, the number of trades open to women in each service expanded rapidly. They included instrument mechanic, searchlight operator, aircraft fitter, balloon rigger, welder and sparkplug tester. By the end of the war, 75 per cent of wireless operators were women, as well as 50 per cent of flight mechanics, 45 per cent of radar operators, and 33 per cent of radar mechanics. At first, the women met suspicion and resistance from men who felt that such trades were not 'women's work', and this meant that women had to work all the harder to prove themselves.

Searchlights in a London park

Angie is a member of a searchlight crew attached to an anti-aircraft battery stationed in the grounds of Allsprings House. Her job was to search the night sky for enemy planes and then to hold them in the beam while the ack-ack guns fired at them. On a mixed anti-aircraft battery, the women operated the equipment to work out the position of the aircraft, but the men fired the guns to shoot them down.

Written work

In pairs. Role play Angie and a journalist for a magazine that is preparing a series of features on women in the forces. First run an interview, then think about how an article on Angie might be written. Will it be a patriotic piece focusing on the good work being done for the war effort? Can the magazine afford to be completely truthful about the women's experiences in the forces? Both write an article and then compare the two.

Drama

1 Imagine that during a re-organisation of the anti-aircraft battery, Angie has requested that she be promoted to the position of gunner. In pairs, improvise the scene in which she makes her request to the battery commander.
2 At the end of the play, the Air-Raid Warden tells Peggy and Liam that the enemy plane crashed into Allsprings House because the guns hit the wing, so preventing the plane from pulling out of a dive. In pairs as the Air-Raid Warden and Angie, role play a scene in which the warden meets Angie after she has taken the Parks children to the station and points out how the plane was brought down. How would Angie react?
3 Two weeks after Rosie and Ben leave, Angie receives notification of posting to another camp. In pairs, improvise a scene in which she tells Peggy the news. Terry is still in the house and no other children have been billeted there since the Parks children left.

LIAM AND DUNKIRK

Very early in the war the British and allied forces in France failed to stop the German advance and it was decided to evacuate the retreating allied soldiers through the French port of Dunkirk. Over 338,000 troops were rescued by naval boats and hundreds of small craft that raced across the channel following an appeal for help. Churchill described Dunkirk as a 'colossal military disaster' and, realising that the Germans might follow the retreating forces across the channel, he prepared the nation to fight on alone:

'...we shall fight on the beaches, we shall fight on the landing grounds, we shall fight in the fields and in the streets, we shall fight in the hills, we shall never surrender...'

Liam tells the story of his part in the Dunkirk evacuation twice in the play. The first is the idealised version that people all over England heard in radio broadcasts and in the newspapers. The second story is closer to the actual experience of the soldiers in retreat, who returned angry and bitter.

In wartime, events are often reported more positively than they actually were in order to boost morale. A disaster may be turned into a triumph, if told in a certain way.

One of the famous radio reports on Dunkirk was made by the writer J B Priestley. He described the special part played in the evacuation by the little seaside pleasure steamers, that normally went no further than the end of the pier:

'These Brighton Belles and Brighton Queens left that innocent, foolish world of theirs to sail into the inferno to defy bombs, shells, magnetic mines, torpedoes, machine-gun fire, to rescue our soldiers. Some of them, alas, will never return.'

One boat that did not return was the *Gracie Fields*, the Isle of Wight ferry boat:

'But now – look – this little steamer, like all her brave and battered sisters, is immortal. She'll go sailing proudly down the years in the epic of Dunkirk. And our great grand children, when they learn how we began this war by snatching glory out of defeat, and then swept on to victory, may also learn how the little holiday steamers made an excursion to hell and came back glorious.'

Discussion

Look carefully at the language that Priestley uses. Why does he describe the boat *Gracie Fields* in this way? His report was heard across the nation. Dunkirk was a major setback early in the war, so *how* he told the story was as important as *what* he told.

Written work

1 Do some research to find out more about what happened at Dunkirk, then imagine that you are an owner of one of the boats that went across the channel, and that you have been asked to write about your experience for the local paper. Write your report in a style similar to that of Liam in his first account of Dunkirk and of J B Priestley's radio broadcast. Focus on one incident, rather than try to cover the whole event.

2 Write another version of the incident including truthful detail you think the editor of the paper would not be prepared to print.

3 Take both reports and divide them into sections, each one about a paragraph in length. Present the reports to the class by reading first a section of one, then a section of the other, alternating the readings till both reports are finished. What is the effect of reading the reports in this way?

THE HOME FRONT

Written work and drama

An interesting way of building a picture of a period of history is to make a radio documentary reporting on characters and events as if everything is taking place in the present.

Many aspects of day to day living during the war are referred to in the play – food rationing, the national 'Dig For Victory' campaign, fears of enemy spies, the blackout, air-raid shelters and air-raid wardens. Together they make a picture of 'The Home Front' – the war at home, which could be the topic of the documentary. A good radio programme requires careful research. Working in small groups, first find out as much as you can about the war at home. Each group could work on one or two topics and become 'expert' in them.

• Look through books and pictures of life during the Second World War (you will find a list of useful titles on page 108).
• Look up copies of wartime newspapers in your local library. Pick out stories and incidents which help to create a picture of home life during the war.
• Talk to people in your area who lived through the war, and, if possible, record their stories.

Your radio documentary will be more exciting if all the voices speak in the present, as if they are living through the war now. This means that the stories you collect from newspapers and local people will have to be adapted so that the voices seem to be talking about the here and now rather than about events in the past.

The voices could include:

1 Different characters speaking directly to the microphone:
   - a housewife describes her problems with the coupons;
   - somebody talks proudly about the beans growing in his window box;
   - an ARP Warden appeals for more care with the blackout;
   - a new recipe using the limited ingredients now available is described;
   - the latest rumour about spies;
   - a mother talks about how she will never spend a night in the Anderson shelters, bombs or no bombs;
   - an evacuee reads a letter she/he has written to send home, or an extract from a daily diary.

2 Overheard conversations:
   - before rationing is introduced two people in a food queue express concern about a well-off person buying up all the sugar (before rationing is introduced);
   - a shopkeeper accuses somebody of rubbing out the crosses (which indicate the ration has already been bought) on the rationing coupons;
   - a Billeting Officer tries to persuade a brother and sister that they must be accommodated in different houses because there are not enough places for them both in one house.

3 Statements of fact:
   - the number of shelters that have been put up in the area;
   - an announcement that all local shops have run out of blackout paper;
   - a new rationing regulation is introduced.

4 Eye witness accounts:
   - a description of a group of evacuees arriving at the station;
   - a false air-raid alarm;
   - a class of schoolchildren being taught how to put their gas masks on.

You could also include the voices of characters from the play – Liam talking about how he thinks Gloria Dawkins will need some help preparing Allsprings House for the evacuees, or the

Billeting Officer expressing disgust about how some mothers show no concern for their evacuated children.

Preparing the documentary

1 Keep each 'voice' fairly short – about 50-60 words.
2 Make sure the voices are varied in character, and that they cover a wide range of topics.
3 Decide on an order for the voices. Some should perhaps be clustered together around a particular topic, in other parts they may gain effect through contrast. Each group may take responsibility for a section of the programme.
4 Make sure that each voice is clear and understandable. Explanations about who is speaking will slow down the documentary and make it less dramatic.
5 All voices should be practised carefully before the recording begins. Try to make each voice flow well and communicate the character of the speaker.

The recording session

All you will need is a recorder with a cassette tape and a microphone. You will probably get the best recording by doing it in one go with everybody concentrating. Find a room which is quiet and where you won't be disturbed. Make sure everybody knows the order of the 'voices' so they will be ready to speak at the right time. Then record each voice in turn. Stop the tape on the pause button as soon as each voice or cluster of voices is finished, and make sure the next voice begins as soon as the pause button is released. In this way you will avoid awkward gaps in the documentary.

When you play the documentary to the class, use a second tape recorder for playing music at the beginning and at the end. With two machines, you will be able to gain effect by cross-fading from one to the other.

EVACUATION STORIES

Involved in the evacuation on 1st September 1939, were
827,000 schoolchildren; 524,000 children under school age
with their mothers; 13,000 expectant mothers; and 103,000
teachers and helpers. In three days, 1,500,000 people were
evacuated. The operation used 3,000 buses, 4,000 trains and
12,000 volunteer helpers.

After their journeys, the evacuees found themselves in
places as far apart as Cornwall, Wales and Cumbria. For
some of them, it was an adventure into a new life they could
never have dreamed of, but for others, it was a miserable and
often frightening experience.

Most of the evacuees came from the poorer parts of towns
and cities, for these were the most densely populated areas.
Families that were better off made their own private
evacuation arrangements.

*'My mother was fed up with packing and unpacking so when
we were told to be ready on the third date given, Mum put a
few clothes in a case. To her horror we were evacuated without
half our belongings.'*

*'We went to school every day with sandwiches, gas-masks
and great big labels. And every day we came back from school
again. We didn't know which day we were being evacuated. So
when I went out to the toilet at the school I saw all these buses
out on the street. So I knew that was going to be the day.'*

Drama

1 Create a scene (with your teacher) in a school classroom
   before the evacuation begins. The teacher enters and
   explains what you will need to bring with you on the
   evacuation. You will have questions you want to ask your
   teacher about where you are going and for how long you will
   be away.
2 In pairs role play a scene in which two parents from
   different families talk about the constant changes in the

arrangements for the evacuation. One is more critical than the other who trusts that the authorities know what they are doing.

3 In the same pairs, role play two mothers from the same street. One likes to think she is posher than her neighbours and talks about 'private arrangements' she has made for getting away; while the other has no choice but to join the government scheme.

4 In groups of four, role play a mother, a father and two children from a poor family. The children have little to take with them and their best clothes are in the pawn shop (a shop which lends you money and keeps valuable belongings of yours until the money is paid back). The mother is worried that she will not be able to provide all the items on the list sent from school. How will her children look if they are billeted with a well-off family?

5 Mothers were very concerned about how their children would cope in their new environment. In pairs, role play a mother and child who have just finished their preparations the night before the evacuation. What advice might the mother give to her child about how to fit in with the new family?

6 Divide into pairs again but with a different partner. Role play a mother and father. The mother is pregnant and has been advised to join the evacuation. The father is an ambulance driver and must stay behind to do war work in the city. The mother is unsure about whether she should go or stay. What might her husband advise her to do?

Written work

Now work on your own. Imagine that you are an evacuee about to leave home. You cannot be certain that you will ever see your home again. In your mind, picture your home - look around it. What special things make it feel like home? Do you have a favourite room? What do you remember of events that have taken place in your home? Write a letter to a person you are leaving behind to be read after you have left.

'When we left we thought we were going to Switzerland because someone mentioned Swindon, and I took my bucket and spade.'

'I recall already sitting on this bus with my two sisters and my mother screaming, "Let Maureen off. Let my baby off. She's too young, she's too young", and they said, "It's too late now, it's too late now", and I can see her running behind the bus screaming, "Betty, don't let them go, don't let them be billeted with anyone else, you've got to look after them, you've got to have them." '

'I was full of beans and I though this is marvellous, it's a lovely day out.'

'We were all put on the buses to Southend station. There we boarded trains. My sister and her friend immediately brought out lipstick and rouge. I was afraid we would be thought of as adults because of the make-up. I remember asking Lila, my sister's friend, why all the people were standing in their gardens waving to us, and she said, "They feel sorry for us. Try to cry, to make it worthwhile." '

'As we pulled away on that rainy morning, leaving my mother on the dock, I think the sense of adventure was replaced by the loneliest feeling in the world, and the wondering of what I was doing there instead of being safe at home with my mum.'

Drama

The train journeys to the new homes were often long and tedious. To relieve the boredom, the evacuees sang songs. One of the most popular was:

Ten green bottles, hanging on the wall
Ten green bottles, hanging on the wall
And if one green bottle should accidentally fall
There'll be nine green bottles, hanging on the wall
Nine green bottles, hanging on the wall
Etc.

If you do not know the tune, your teacher will. Try singing the song as a whole class. Then sing it again as evacuees on the train, but this time pause at the end of each verse. In the silences, one evacuee in the train speaks his/her inner thoughts about what they are leaving behind or about what is to come. Try to build a dramatic tension between the jollity of the song and the 'silent' thoughts of the singers.

RECEPTION AND BILLETING

The arrival of evacuees in the reception towns and villages was chaotic. In some places larger numbers of evacuees than expected arrived and school halls had to be opened up in which beds were hastily assembled. In other places, grand receptions were laid on but only a handful of children arrived. Some welcoming parties, expecting to entertain only children, found themselves with mothers and babies and pregnant women. All who arrived, young and old, were tired, dirty and hungry.

The 'cattle market'

There then followed what was for many, the worst experience of the whole evacuation. Some called it the 'cattle market'. This was the process of sorting out which adults were going to take which children. Sometimes this took place on the railway platform, but usually the evacuees were taken to a dispersal centre where the 'auction' began.

'I remember crying because I thought a strange looking man with watery eyes was going to take us home.'

'We had to stand in rows for absolutely ages while posh-talking women armed with notebooks and pens walked along the lines of us evacuees and selected ones and twos.'

'One little girl was in tears because no one would have her and she came to me and said, "Doesn't anyone want me?"'

Drama

1 Imagine the scene on the station platform where lots of evacuees have arrived and the billeting officers are struggling to cope with the chaos. People have arrived to take the evacuees and are talking among themselves or to the billeting officer. In pairs or groups of three, create short snippets of their conversations – e.g. a farmer and his wife look for a strong boy to work on their farm, a man needs a 'good, helpful girl' to help his wife who has just had a baby, a local big-wig tries to make up his mind which is the prettiest of two girls, a woman has chosen an evacuee, but then sees a pair of 'darling twins' and changes her mind.

2 What might the children have been thinking when all this was going on around them? Imagine yourself as an evacuee sitting cross-legged on the floor waiting to be picked out. Speak your thoughts to yourself about the people you see around you. How can you tell who might be the sort of people you could live with?

3 If the parents of the evacuees could see the scene, what would they say? In pairs as the mother and father of evacuated children, make statements in turn about what you see (without interacting with the scene). Comments may be about the adults, or advice to the child, or instructions to the Billeting Officer.

4 You now have three elements which could be used for a more extended drama – snatches of dialogue, thoughts of the evacuees, comments by the parents. Try putting them together to create a dramatic impression of the 'cattle market'. Make each section or statement quite short, and build variety and contrast into the sequence.

5 *'We were told to sit quietly on the floor while the villagers and farmers' wives came to choose which children they wanted. I noticed boys of about 12 went very quickly – perhaps to help on the farm? Eventually only my friend Nancy and myself were left – two plain, straight-haired little girls wearing glasses, now rather tearful.'*

In groups of four, role play the two girls mentioned above, a lady who has come to take some evacuees and the Billeting Officer. The lady claims that she had her name down for two boys, but the Officer can't provide them: it's these two or nothing. If the lady takes them home, how might her husband react to the two girls?

6 In groups of six, role play a brother and sister, the Billeting Officer, and 3 householders. The two evacuees, following their mother's advice, have refused to be separated but have not yet been found a home. The Billeting Officer takes them along a street knocking on doors seeking accommodation for them, but each house has a different reason for not taking them.

NEW FAMILIES

Most foster families welcomed new guests into their homes with warmth, patience and affection.

Arrival at the billet

'They were two of the poorest little scraps of humanity you could imagine. They were dressed in what had once been blue velvet dresses, much washed and faded, several sizes too big, that reached down to their ankles – and the extra width was taken up with two large safety pins, centre waist! They wore a pair of navy knickers each – minus elastic – plimsolls, and grey socks, which at some stage had once been white. To top this, there were two little, thin, drawn, tear-stained faces – tired, bewildered and very insecure. All they had was what they stood up in.' (foster mother)

Drama

1 Divide into groups of four and role play a foster mother and father, and two evacuees. The hosts have prepared a special welcome tea and they are anxious that their new children will settle in quickly and be happy (perhaps they never had any children of their own, and this is the first time they have a 'family'). The evacuees feel very strange in the house and are not sure how to behave. Some of the food they have never seen before. Improvise the scene in which the foster parents and evacuees share their first meal.

2 Try the scene again but with a difference. The evacuees, against all the rules, have concealed a pet in a box under the stairs, and it needs feeding. How might they take food from the table during tea without the new foster parents noticing?

3 A few days later in the same house, bed-wetting has become a serious problem (as it was for many evacuees). The mother and father talk over what to do about it. What might they say to the evacuees to help solve the problem?

4 In groups of four, read the story below from an evacuee called Sheila, and then the letter sent by a mother to a women's magazine.

'As our transport delivered us to our prospective houses, it was with great awe that I encountered my fairy-tale house. A distinguished, white-haired gentleman met us at Foston House. His warmth and genial hospitality afforded such comfort. This I never forgot.

Colonel Drew was a widower and had lost a daughter aged 20. He was also Magistrate at Stoke Poges. There were six of us from my school.

The orchard bore fruit, we had a car to take us to school, a piano, a beautiful home, servants, typing lessons, mini-golf and a fine lawn. Most of all we had met warmth and understanding, for us poor children, cast into the country by the fate of war.

Such a happy life I had found, though Mother never strayed from my thoughts nor indeed my whole family. My father came on leave and I was very proud of him in his uniform. However, he could be a 'know-it-all' and I must confess I felt a little ashamed at his first meeting with Colonel Drew. For in my eyes 'mine host' was far superior. Years later as I write, I can now see – perhaps my father was right. He was a good man.

The education, kindness and the insight to a 'better' life brought with it a change in me. I became a snob...but still caring for those at home.'

Anxious Mother

We have let our only girl be evacuated with her school, and she has had the luck to get into a very good home. But one thing is troubling us. We live very simply in a three-roomed flat, and where she is there are many servants. From her letters I can see she is thrilled about all this. She is thirteen, and we are afraid it will make her quite dissatisfied with our ways.

Yes, I understand your anxiety, but could you not look at it in another way? Your child will get advantages – think what it will mean to her health in the coming winter. Even though temporarily she may have a 'swelled head', this is certain to adjust itself. I am sure you are glad that your daughter is not in a crowded home. Don't be afraid, but welcome the fact that she is cared for.

(letter from Mother & Home women's magazine)

Drama

Now imagine that the letter was written by Sheila's mother and that sometime after the letter to the magazine both parents decided to take up an invitation from Colonel Drew to visit Foston House. How might Sheila react to her parents in her new home? In a group of four, improvise the visit. This could be divided into different scenes:

1 The Colonel's chauffeur and Sheila meet her parents at the station.
2 The chauffeur now changes role to the Colonel. After a tour around the grounds, the Colonel, Sheila and her parents take tea on the veranda. Sheila's parents are quite overwhelmed by the surroundings.
3 The Colonel leaves Sheila with her parents for a while before they depart. Her parents tell her that no bombs have fallen yet, so there is a good chance that Sheila may be able to come home soon. How would Sheila feel about returning home?

Written work

1 Many inner city children experienced the joys and 'fears' of the countryside for the first time. Imagine yourself to be one

of these children. Up till now, all you have known about the country is what you have seen in books. But here you are in the real countryside. What do you notice first? What things take you by surprise? Write down your thoughts and reaction to what you see.

2 By no means all the children who were evacuated came from poor homes. Suppose that two of you have been evacuated from London where you have been used to modern conveniences. Now you find yourselves on a farm in Cornwall where there is no running water, and the toilet is behind the house. You are both in bed and it is dark and windy outside. Everyone in the house is asleep. One of you begins to feel sick...Now continue the story.

Written work and drama

Though most evacuees were treated well by their new foster parents, some had traumatic experiences.

'Her favourite punishment was to lock us in a cupboard under the stairs (where there was no light) without supper. It is hard to know whether the hunger or the dark held more horrors for me.'

Some evacuees escaped and travelled long distances back home.

'At London Bridge Station I found a train going to Croydon, and as I had been travelling for about 12 hours by now, I just told the guard at the gate that I had no money and he held on to me until just before the train started, then handed me over to the guard with instructions to put me off at Croydon station.

Having got off I had about a two-mile walk to my house in the dark. When I got home my mother came to the door and to my amazement said, "What are you doing here?" and slapped me!'

Invent your own escape story. You could either write it, or act it out, or both. The story will be more dramatic if it includes a picture of life in the foster home before you escape. Remember that, in drama, events do not need to played in the order that they happen. So, for example, scenes about the foster home, rather then being placed at the start of the play, could be slotted in between scenes of the return home. How will you travel without money? What will you eat? Your journey will be full of adventure and danger, and unexpected things may happen.

THE BLITZ

During the first raid on London in September 1940, hundreds of German bombers dropped high explosive and incendiary bombs killing 430 people and injuring 1600. Attacks followed on Coventry, the southern ports of Southampton, Portsmouth, and Plymouth, and later, on the industrial towns of the north, Manchester, Merseyside, Hull, and Glasgow in Scotland.

London burns

Explosive bombs varied in weight from 50 to 2,500 kilograms. A blast would tear everything around to shreds, rip gaping holes in the ground, and throw vehicles high into the air. Incendiary bombs were each about the size of a wine bottle and weighed no more than a couple of pounds. They fell in clusters, clattering on the roof tops, then they began to burn and set fire to buildings. The fires burned with such intensity, that the incendiary bombs often caused more damage than the explosive bombs.

Explosive bombs came down making a terrifying whistling sound, convincing people that the bomb was heading straight for them.

'My, when I heard that awful whistling...I went sort of numb. This is it, I thought; this is what it feels like when it gets you, all sort of numb. It seemed to be coming right at us, dead straight, right at this house...I couldn't credit it this morning when they told me it had fallen on the Grange (cinema, half a mile away).'

Though the sirens warned of approaching planes, it wasn't always possible to get to the shelter on time. Like Liam and Gloria at the end of the play, some people found themselves stranded.

'There was the oddest feeling in the air, all around, it was as if the whole air was falling apart, quite silently...and then, suddenly, I was on my face; just inside the kitchen door. There seemed to be waves buffeting me, one after another, like bathing in a rough sea. I remember clutching the floor – the carpet, or something – to prevent myself being swept away.'

As people emerged from the shelters after the raid, they would be thinking – has the house been hit? Who's been killed? How will we cope?

It is said that after a direct experience of bombing, people go through various stages of adjustment.

Stage 1 (first few minutes) Shock – no feelings of fear or pain.

Stage 2 (next 1 or 2 hours) A sense of reality returns. They feel concern for others and worry about the damage done. They have a first awareness of any injuries or pain.

Stage 3 (following hours) They exchange personal experiences saying the same things over and over and they feel intense excitement.

Stage 4 (next 48 hours) They have feelings of pride in people and in the neighbourhood.

Stage 5 (after 48 hours) Return to normal.

Written work

1 Imagine that you have been in a shelter during a heavy air-raid. The planes have now gone, the bombs have stopped and the ALL CLEAR has sounded. Write down the reactions you feel as you emerge from the shelter and see the damage all around. It may help to write your feelings at different points in time to fit with the stages of adjustment (page 98).
2 After completing the first draft, try expressing the feelings in a poem. Each stage of adjustment could form a separate section of your poem.
3 Evacuees away from home would fear for the safety of their parents when they heard about raids on their home town or city. Try this writing exercise in pairs: one of you is an evacuee away from home, the other a parent who has stayed behind. There is an air raid on the home neighbourhood. The evacuee has heard about the raid, but does not know any details. The parent has survived but is not sure how much of the truth to tell. Each write a letter to the other. The letters 'cross in the post' and are then read at the same time. After completing the writing and reading, discuss in your pairs the decisions you made about what to put in and what to leave out of the letter.

SCHOOLS IN THE BLITZ

During the first few months of the war, the enemy bombers did not arrive as expected, and many evacuees drifted back home. Schools in areas that had been evacuated (except the areas of highest risk) had to be re-opened. All the schools had shelters and the pupils practised the air-raid drill regularly. School shelters had wooden benches, and boxes of books, comics and sweets to keep the children occupied until the ALL CLEAR sounded. Some schools were hit in daylight raids, and many children were killed.

In the play, Margaret's story about her friend Frances is based on a true incident which took place on 20 January 1943 at Sandford Road School in Catford, London. On that day, the barrage balloons, which normally were flown over the city to prevent enemy planes from flying low, had been taken down for inspection. This gave the raiders an unexpected opportunity to fly low over the streets and aim their bombs with precision.

In the school, the top class were in the hall having their lunch, and another class were lining up to leave for a special visit to the theatre to see a performance of *A Midsummer Night's Dream* by Shakespeare. Lots of other children were in the playground. For some reason the air-raid siren close to the school was not sounded even though the siren in the adjoining area had gone off. Some people in the Catford area heard this siren in the distance, but in the school, with the noise of the children in the playground, nobody noticed it in time to warn everbody to get to the shelters. 38 pupils and 6 teachers died in the raid.

Casualties in the school playground

A German Evacuation Story

In the horror and destruction of war, it is easy to take a one-sided view and blame everything on the enemy. But it is important to remember that while German bombers were inflicting death and destruction over Britain, British aircraft were devastating German cities, killing many thousands of civilians. In 1943, a blanket bombing raid (when so many planes drop bombs that they cover the entire city like a blanket) on the northern German city of Hamburg created a gigantic firestorm which burnt the whole city and killed 42,000 people. Later in the war, a similar attack on Dresden caused more deaths than the atomic bomb on Hiroshima in Japan in 1945.

The first attempt by British Bomber Command to destroy a large city by blanket bombing took place on the night of 30 May, 1942. The target was Cologne. 1,046 British planes took part in the raid. The number of German deaths, about 500, was small in relation to the massed bomber raids to follow, but 45,000 people lost their homes. Heidi Prüfer was one of them. She lived in Cologne with her four children – two girls and two boys.

Heidi Prüfer

Heidi had already lost her husband in the war. In the blanket bombing raid, her house was hit by incendiary bombs and burned to the ground. She lost everything, but survived and went to live with her parents. The air raids became more frequent and Heidi decided to move with her children to a safe evacuation area. This is her story.

'We all boarded the train that was to take us to an evacuation address in Thuringia. There was no heating on the train. The water in the pipes was all frozen. Babies started crying. On the journey we were attacked by low-flyers.

It was already dark and freezing cold by the time we reached our destination of Walldorf an der Werra, but at least we should be safe from the bombers here. We disembarked at the station, too weary to talk, and were greeted by the local Hitler Youth, who sang songs and played guitars as we walked into the little town...

We were taken to a school. The largest of the classrooms had been laid out with straw, and there all the people from the train bedded down, men and women, old and young together.

Over the next few days the evacuees were allocated to different families in the neighbourhood. No luck for us, though.

Wilfried, my second youngest, had in the meantime made firm friends with a fat lady who had a loaf of bread hidden in her coat pocket and kept giving him pieces. He couldn't resist bread, and refused to be parted from her.

The Gauleiter (Nazi district official) said to me, "Make out you've only got two children, and then we'll take it from there." And that is how we managed to get a room in a house owned by an elderly couple. I took the two girls with me, whilst the boys had to go somewhere else.

Heidi's sons, Gunther aged 6, and Wilfred, aged 7

Later I made my little confession, and was allowed to have the boys join us. There was just the one room, a bit on the small side for the five of us. There was no proper bed and just one of those cylindrical iron stoves, which had to serve us for heating, cooking and washing...it was a strain living there in a completely strange environment, amongst complete strangers. They never made us exactly welcome and seemed to regard taking us in as a bothersome duty.'

Written work

1 Imagine that you are Heidi searching through the charred remains of your house after the bombing raid. What do you find? A toy perhaps, or a book with a message inside. What memories do they evoke of your family and of the times you have spent together?

2 Now you find one object that is special. Picture a particular moment in the past which explains why the object means so much to you. Write a poem about this moment.

Drama

1 In groups of five, create a still tableau of Heidi's family huddled together on the cold train.

2 There are other people on the train who have been affected by the war. Who are they? What do you imagine has been their experience of the war? In the same group of five, create a second tableau depicting the other passengers.

3 Imagine that all the passengers have now arrived at the school and are preparing beds on the straw that has been laid on the floor. They begin to exchange their stories and their reasons for coming to the evacuation centre. Build a scene around this situation.

4 In pairs. A few days have passed and most people have found accommodation with families, but Heidi and her children are still at the school. Nobody wants the burden of so many mouths to feed. Heidi has just been advised to pretend she only has two children. She is feeling desperate when another person arrives to take some evacuees. Role play Heidi's conversation with this person.

5 Heidi and her two girls are now lodging with a family, but they are treated as a 'bothersome duty'. Working in groups of five, role play Heidi, the two girls and two members of the

other family. Choose one incident where Heidi is made to feel particularly unwelcome, and then act it out. How do her children react during the incident?

6 The family has agreed to the two boys joining Heidi and the girls in the house, but Heidi has no money left. In groups of three, role play Heidi and the couple who own the house she is staying in. How might Heidi ask them for a small loan to buy food for her children who are continually hungry?

7 It is night and Heidi lies awake, unable to sleep. The only sound is the ticking of a clock. Heidi's thoughts drift back to times past when her husband was alive and her family lived together in their own house. Choose a moment that Heidi remembers, and in small groups, bring it to life in action. Make the memory short, like a glimpse from a longer scene that Heidi is thinking about. It will help you if you are clear in your own mind why Heidi has remembered it. Link the memories that each group comes up with by performing them in sequence around a tableau of Heidi's family asleep in the bedroom. Between the performance of each memory the focus could return to the bedroom and the ticking clock. Create the mood carefully – the still silence of night-time, Heidi awake in the dark, unfamiliar house, thinking and remembering.

Heidi Prüfer and all her children survived the war. As soon as it was safe to do so, they made the long journey home:

'We were all filthy dirty, and, once we got to the opposite bank of the Rhine, one of our prams decided to give up the ghost. We got a lift on a gas-powered truck and it took us right to the door of my parents' house. My mother almost fainted with relief at the sight of us all. Thank God, we'd all survived! What more could we ask?'

HOW TO BUILD YOUR OWN PLAY ABOUT THE EVACUATION

If you have worked through the practical ideas suggested in the previous sections, you will have created enough characters and scenes to build your own play about the evacuation. Putting a play together is not as difficult as it may seem. As in the actual evacuation, your play can involve many different people and stories. The following practical steps will help you to build the play. Read through all the steps before you start any practical work.

1 Decide which scenes should be acted by the whole group – for example, a class assembling in the school playground before departure or evacuees arriving at their destination. Make a list of these scenes, but do not rehearse them yet.

2 Now divide into groups of five or six. Each group should then work independently on scenes requiring only a few characters. Choose scenes from any part of the evacuation. In some scenes you will need all five/six people, but you can also subdivide the group for scenes requiring only twos or threes. Include at least one scene in which a character speaks his/her thoughts directly to the audience.

3 In your choice of scenes, variety and contrast in atmosphere and intensity will be more important that a connected story-line. Do not worry if the situations you have chosen seem similar to those in other groups, you will find that, in performance, scenes based on the same idea can be quite different. At the end of the rehearsal process, make a list of all the scenes you have created in your group.

4 In order to stage the play you will need a large performance area, preferably the school hall. Rather than use one acting area for all the scenes, give each sub-group its own area

around a central acting space. This will allow the drama to change from one location to another without a break.

5 With the whole class together, allocate a performance area to each group. With the help of your teacher, decide the order of the scenes to be performed. Bear in mind the importance of building dramatic contrast into the sequence – for example, a large group scene followed by a quiet scene between two characters or a serious incident followed by humorous dialogue. Make sure that no two scenes by the same sub-group are placed together as this will cause awkward scene changes which will slow down the performance.

6 At this point, you may want to think about adapting one of the small group scenes to involve the whole group – for example, a 'cattle market' scene. If so, keep the characters and shape of the scene as devised, but use the rest of the class as 'extras'.

7 Now go back to the large group scenes and rehearse them. Decide which acting space each of them will use.

8 Give each scene a name and number and make a new list of scenes in the order you have decided to perform them.

9 Collect costumes and props that will help to give the play a feel of the war period. If possible, light each acting area with a spotlight, but keep all technical preparations to a minimum. Good acting and ensemble work will give the drama a more authentic feel than technical accuracy. Look ahead for practical problems that may arise. Avoid complicated scene shifts and changes.

10 Make sure that each scene in the play is carefully rehearsed. You could start and end each scene with a frozen image.

11 You are now almost ready to perform your play. But first check that everybody knows:
  • the number of each scene in which they perform;
  • which performance areas they will be using;
  • where props and costumes are placed.
Each group should have a copy of the scene list for reference.

12 Now the performance can begin. While each group is performing, the next group should be setting up.

13 Your teacher could indicate on card or the blackboard the number of each scene as it is performed. This will help you to keep track of what is happening and to know what you should be doing.

14 Avoid awkward gaps by making sure that each new scene starts as soon as the previous one is finished.

15 In this staging design, the audience has no fixed location but follows the play to each acting area where the scenes are taking place, either standing or sitting for the duration of the scene. This helps the audience to feel part of the action, especially in the whole group scenes which are performed in the central area.

This is a rough and ready method of building a play, but it will give you a broad picture of the work you have created. Part of the fun is seeing the work of other groups in a shared performance. After the first run through, it is likely that you will see many ways in which the play could be improved. You may wish to cut some scenes because they repeat ideas in other scenes, or to develop particular characters, or to build in music and sound effects to link the scenes.

To give the drama a sharper focus you could:

1 Concentrate on two or three contrasting evacuee stories.
   story 1 – a poor child billeted with a well-off family
   story 2 – a brother and sister are cruelly treated by foster parents and plan an escape
   story 3 – a German evacuee story

2 Develop a single evacuation story.
   Many years after the war, some evacuees returned to the places where they had been evacuated to try to remember what it was like, and, perhaps, to meet old friends:
   'Kathy is still a great pal and when I went down last she took me around to the school. The school hadn't altered at all and she said, "I want to show you something". Tears came to my eyes as she lifted the desk-top. Our names were still written on it.'
   One way of structuring a play about a single evacuation story would be to begin in the present with an evacuee, now an adult, returning to the village that he/she was evacuated to as a child. As he/she walks around the village, memories and feelings return.

BOOKS FOR FURTHER READING AND RESEARCH

For information about the evacuation and life during the war:
No Time To Wave Goodbye, by Ben Wicks (Bloomsbury)
The Day They Took The Children, by Ben Wicks (Bloomsbury)
(Most of the quotes of evacuees used in this book were taken from the above)
Living Through The Blitz, by Tom Harrisson (Penguin)
The People's War: Britain 1939-45, by Angus Calder (The Literary Guild)
London At War: The Hulton-Deutsch Collection, by Clive Hardy and Nigel Arthur (Quoin)
The People's War, by Juliet Gardiner (Collins and Brown)
The Day War Broke Out, by Peter Haining (W H Allen)
The Home Front: The Best of Good Housekeeping 1939-45, compiled by Brian Braithwaite, Noelle Walsh, Glyn Davies (Ebury Press)

Novels set in the Second World War:
Goodnight, Mr Tom, by Michelle Magorian (Penguin)
Carrie's War, by Nina Bawdon (Puffin Books/Victor Gollancz)
No Shelter, by Elizabeth Lutzeier (Collins Cascades Series)
In Spite of All Terror, by Hester Burton (O. U. P.)
Fireweed, by Jill Paton Walsh (Puffin Books)